I0710852

The Browser IExodus 20-01-17

The Greatest Social Science Data Collection Since the Library of Alexandria

Erik A Brunau

Copyright 2020

"Advance the upright and set aside the crooked, then the people will submit. Advance the crooked and set aside the upright then the people will not submit." Confucius pp. 12 from the Four Books

Table of Contents

When I Was a Kid ...

"Hey, who wants to ride down to George's ?" Seriously, just down the road, you find the childhood home of George Abbott, the author of <u>Damn Yankees</u>. Grammie Abbott would always tell me to write it down. Grammie said, "George spent a lot of time sitting under the tree writing instead of working on the land." I remember going to Grammie and asking, "If grown-ups can adopt little people, can little people adopt Grammies?" Grammie Abbott paused with a look, smiled, and said, "Why yes, of course, you can." I then asked her, "Can I adopt you as my Grammie?" She said, "Yes." She became my Grammie Abbott just like that and made the best baked-beans ever! She always said to make sure your dinner plate has a lot of color on it. The stories she could tell about the Fair, the Pierce-Arrow Company, Pierce Avenue, and the Trolley Tracks. The Farmers Market and the Hitching Post, the Confederate money in the old farmhouse walls, Flappers, Woodrow Wilson, and "the Amendment was giving women the Right to Vote," little White Boxing Gloves, and brewing beer during Prohibition. The Sacred Burial Grounds along Clark Street and Miss Kitty from Gunsmoke at the Union Street School!

George's Hotdog's Let's go! We all looked at each other, waited a moment; we had to ask our moms, mine a beautician, our fathers were at work. We jumped on our bikes, pedaling as fast as we could to ask our moms. We also had to get $1.50 out of our allowance for our hot dog, burger, fries, pop, or shake and let her know we arrived calling from the payphone at the new B-Kwik on Abbott Road. We all met up at the trail and headed into the woods towards the ravine. It was a small trail with swinging vines, deer sometimes, slate rocks, and water coming down from the spring.

The paths were well worn; at times, though, you had to navigate using common sense, the sun, and moss on the tree.

Parents were not on speed dial; GPS was for the Gemini-Apollo Missions. We did not have 3, 5, 10, or 15 different gears on our bikes. It was coaster brakes and a steep downhill ride at 11 or 10 yrs of age! Those Western Flyer bike shock absorbers were either the padding on your seat, the fat on your butt, or standing up on your pedals using your knee absorbers. It is about a 2.5 mile trip by car; Uber-Lyft service was not an option; by bike, you could cut half the distance going through the woods. We would get to the bottom of the hill, and our chains might be a tad loose. If the chains fell off, we would flip our bikes upside down and spin them back on. Everyone had eaten their lunch we headed back up the hill! We would spend the next 5-6 weeks talking about the bike ride. We earned twenty-five cents a week for doing our chores.

All the student's eyes glued to the front of the room until that fingernail scratch across the chalkboard. The putrid aroma of rotten eggs filling the classroom from the Bunson burner stands by the exit door. The sight of his Pall Mall cigarette smoke rising from his mouth, the last puff from his desk, walking, the sound of hacking and spitting his phlegm into the vast deep sink. A memory recall, "I am Mr. Walter, your Science teacher, and we are going to learn about electricity." It was my first "F-Fail." The U.S. Navy determining I had a superior aptitude in electronics and motor mechanics based on the Armed Services Vocational Aptitude Battery (ASVAB) test, go figure! The live mice are sitting in fish-tanks along the window panes awaiting their turn in the smoke chamber before lung dissection.

Yes, Mr. Walter was a real Science Teacher. The mice were indeed contributions to lung cancer research at Roswell Park Research Center. How many heard the scratch on the chalkboard and cringed in response? Did you smell rotten eggs? How many ran to the "Lav" for a smoke between Class? Who is offended and experiencing a sense of disgust to the smoker's cough? Dry cough, hacking, and spitting phlegm into the classroom sink? Symptoms of? Does anyone feel concerned for the mice or the nightly janitor cleaning up the Science room? Who can navigate the woods without GPS? Fear of being lost in the woods? Hitch the horse team? These emotional responses, their visualization, are the target of digital replication, their trigger point within your brain mapped and entered into human-computer interaction system databases throughout the world. *This input collected from every web site, every game played, every purchase, every phone call, every email, every digital interaction you have had since AOL, and before said "You've Got Mail" to you.* This data is being cataloged, creating a Personal Digital Record (PDR). Creating machines with the likeness of their real-world male human image is a directive for modern Artificial Intelligence Object-Oriented Programming (AIOOP) or Artificial Intelligence Procedural Programming (AIPP).

Luckin, Rose; Holmes, Wayne; Griffiths, Mark, and Forcier, Laurie B. (2016) identify a mapping process to adjust and accommodate our education system for the future. The full integration of Artificial Intelligence to educate future generations is possible and for each student, a personal tutor. This tutor requires a system capable of executing the principles of learning (Skinner, Bloomberg Taxonomy, Piaget, Vygotsky), input to create curriculum (Subject Matter Experts), and design programs explicitly created for each student. We need to identify the skillsets required in the AI environment while we exist in this transitional state of Tech. We are moving from driving a car toward it drives us, the optional mandate for homeschool using the Internet versus traditional classroom. A current pandemic is providing an opportunity for parents, students, educators, and administrators to gather feedback on how to improve the student experience. Prodigy has some exciting and seemingly affordable programs for essential reading, writing, and arithmetic at this URL: https://www.prodigygame.com/blog/educational-games-for-kids/ . This learning environment seems different than Grammie or Mr. Walter's classroom, even my own in this story. The future is ...

AIEd models	What the model represents	Examples of specific knowledge represented in AIEd models
Pedagogical model	The knowledge and expertise of teaching	'Productive failure' (allowing students to explore a concept and make mistakes before being shown the 'right' answer)
		Feedback (questions, hints, or haptics), triggered by student actions, which is designed to help the student improve their learning
		Assessment to inform and measure learning
Domain model	Knowledge of the subject being learned (domain expertise)	How to add, subtract, or multiply two fractions
		Newton's second law (forces)
		Causes of World War I
		How to structure an argument
		Different approaches to reading a text (e.g. for sense or for detail)
Learner model	Knowledge of the learner	The student's previous achievements and difficulties
		The student's emotional state
		The student's engagement in learning (for example: time-on-task)

Figure 1: Luckin, Rose; Holmes, Wayne; Griffiths, Mark and Forcier, Laurie B. (2016). Intelligence Unleashed: An Argument for AI in Education. Pearson Education, London. pp 19

The first course I experienced that required using a computer was Behavioral Statistics somewhere between 1982-1985. I hated using the computer. Research often attributed this discomfort to computer anxiety, where it was initiating humanity to accept an artificial significant other. I did have an IBM typewriter with limited memory and only allowed three "white-outs" per typed page or term paper. The first computer I owned was a Tandy 1000 or T2000 around 1987. The word processor program with spell check was a must-have in Graduate School. I remember getting my first Windows 95 Computer, and "Q" provided the tour. Initially, I could not figure out how to turn it on. I still have it in my home. It has no monitor, still have the speakers, the mic, but lost the start-up 3 1/2 inch disks. Today, you can download Win95 as an "app." I did perform a fresh install without much use before purchasing a Win 98. It will power up, but a hard shut down is not recommended for it today. I switched to XP and still have startup disks with the license codes to them. Then, I had a leftover Window ME and learned about Linux OS! KDE running on OpenSuSE, Canonical, and Fedora for free, cheap laptops and desktops. Motorola Droid A1 was a great phone, easy to root, replacing the user interface and OS. The Motorola Droid Bionic required using Linux to root. Computer building today is natural. Basics you need a case, motherboard, processor, hard drive, power source, a free OS resulting in a new computer. Today, I use either Linux or Windows.

The first programming language I learned was Pascal. C, Java, and SQL followed it. The first program I learned to write is "Hello World" in C. It has a header file, Main function, a function call, and a return. C is a procedural language; you have to perform each code statement in a logical step-by-step process from beginning to end. You have to use the correct punctuation to terminate a Statement. There is a massive difference between a period and a comma. Programming in C is like chaining a behavior using Behavior Modification. The output to the screen is simple stimulus, response, and the end product is the reward. Object-oriented programming approaches programming by treating the code

```c
// Simple C program to display "Hello World"

// Header file for input output functions
#include <stdio.h>

// main function -
// where the execution of program begins
int main()
{

    // prints hello world
    printf("Hello World");

    return 0;
}
```

Figure 2: Hello World in C

as a person, place, or thing termed a Class. Then, you have assignments statement and function calls, which are the static and movement of the Class. Then, a Class can instantiate as many cars, dogs, airplanes, or space ships as desired. They are similar to the difference between psychology and sociology observation and creation. *Is this programming a machine or conditioning the mind and behavior of a programmer? Human beings?*

AI could be considered any software program written to assist humans with the desired task. For example, CDBurner XP initialized in 2003 designed as a free alternative to create CD, DVD, and ISO. Then, in 2008, "Help Files" for many programs were not easy for users without a computer background to understand. Help4Software created a visual step by step in learning how to use the application. These "Help Files" a series of "screenshots" with arrows or small videos presented in a consecutive order toward completion of the task. *Procedural Programming?* These "Help Files" were loaded into Wiki for future users to access.

CDBurnerXP

Software

Figure 3: CDBurner XP https://cdburnerxp.se/en/home

The eCounty Holding Inmate Release Protocol System (eCHIRPS) was a single attempt to create a web-based system to handle the criminal justice and corrections booking system over ten years ago. The system at the county was outdated and insufficient, leaving it primed for errors and media attention. It presented an enormous challenge and opportunity to practice new skill sets in Web Base Programming and Database Design. It would have been better as a Graduate Programming Course Exercise versus a Just for Fun Project! These screenshots provide a small glimpse into the magnitude of this type of project, the database size, and the type of data that is potentially collected in similar systems today.

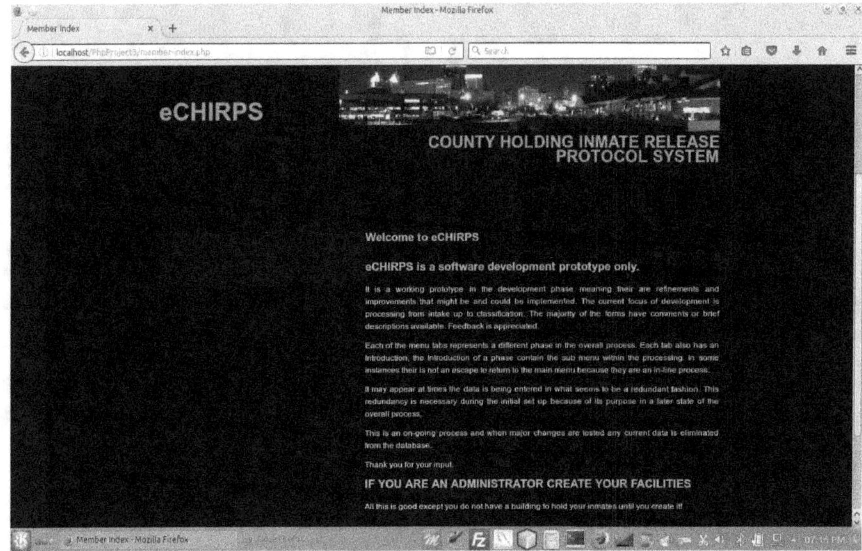

Figure 4: eCHIRP Welcome Screen After Log-In

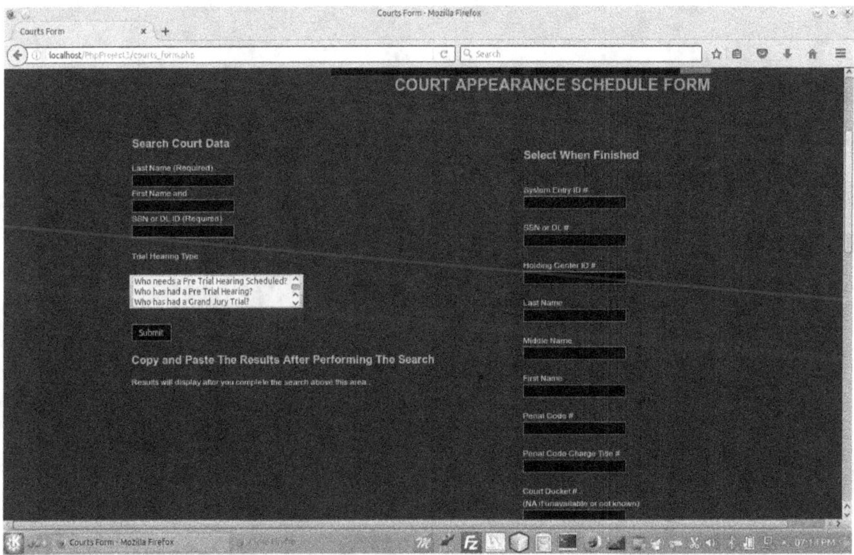

Figure 5: eCHIRP Court Scheduling Status

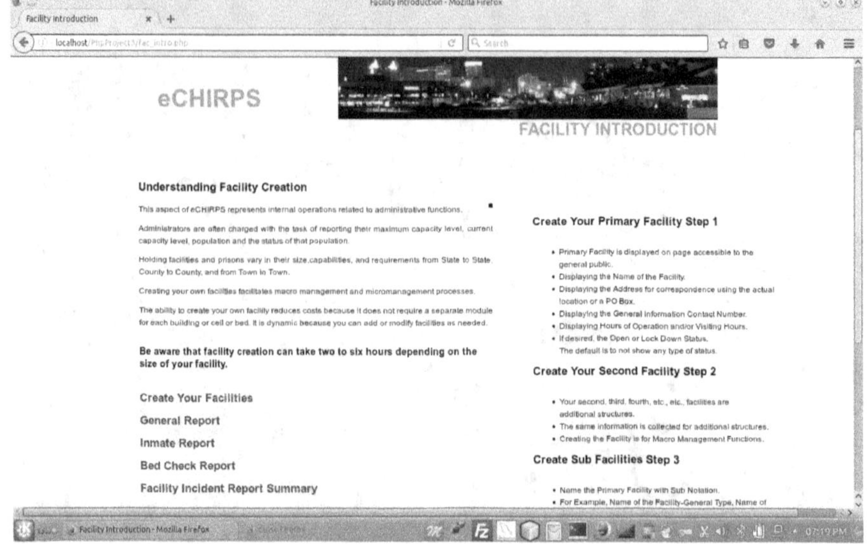

Figure 6: eCHIRP Holding Facility Creation

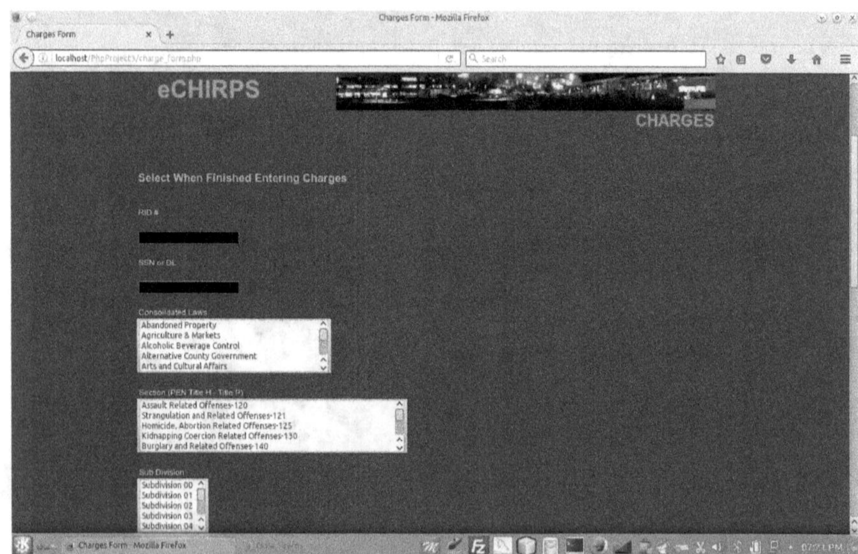

Figure 7: eCHIRP NYS Criminal Codes at Date of Creation

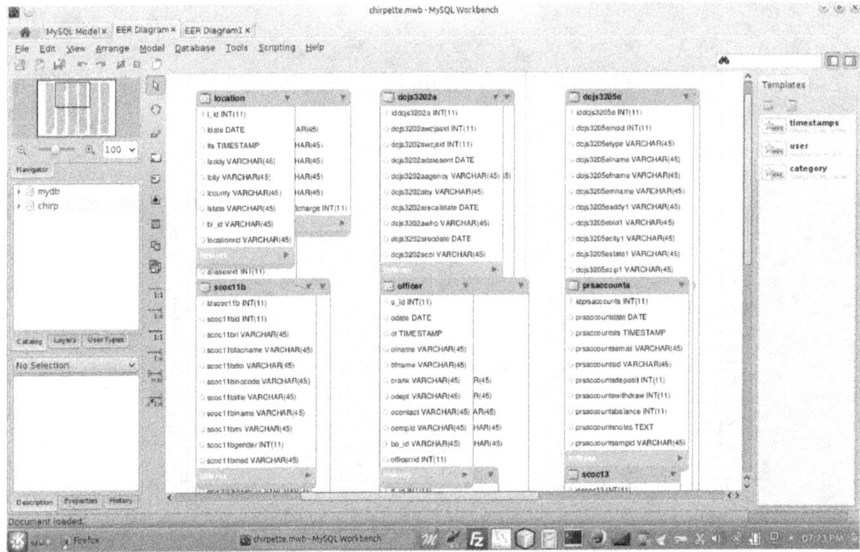

Figure 8: eCHIRP Database Visual Design (Partial)

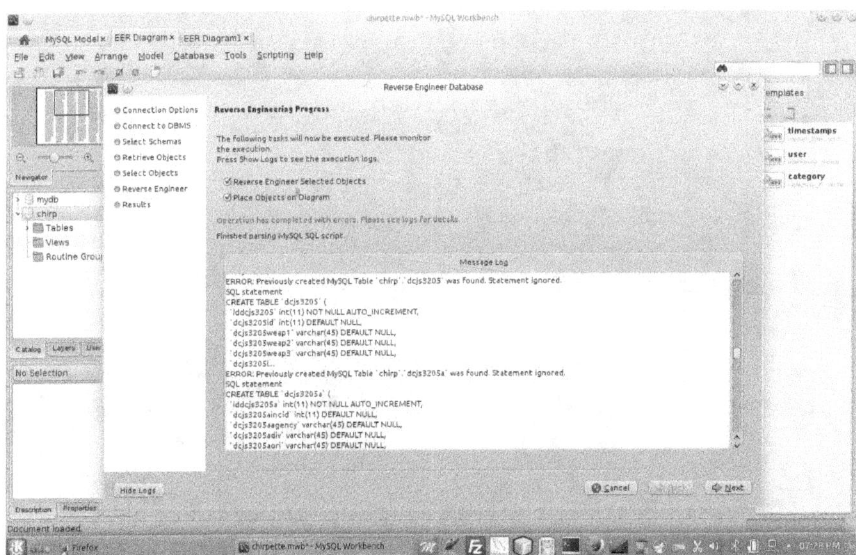

Figure 9: eCHIRP SQL Code (Partial)

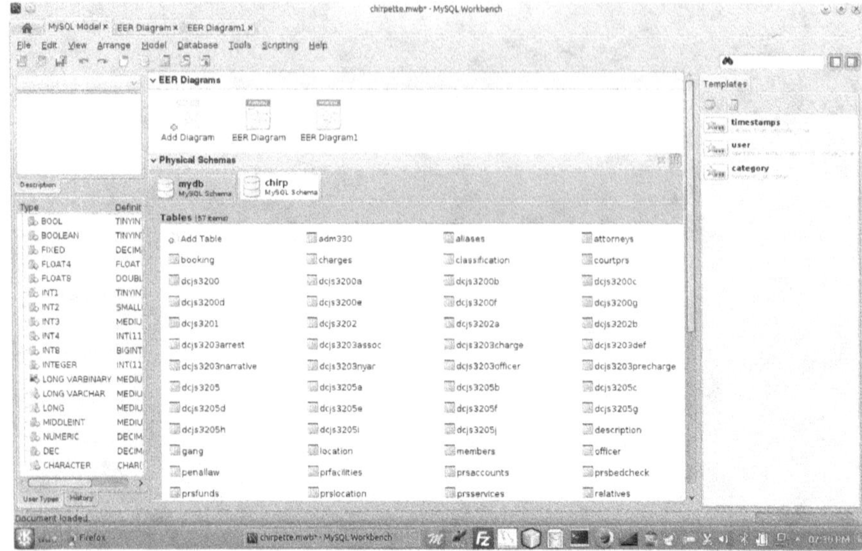

Figure 10: eCHIRPS Database Tables (Partial)

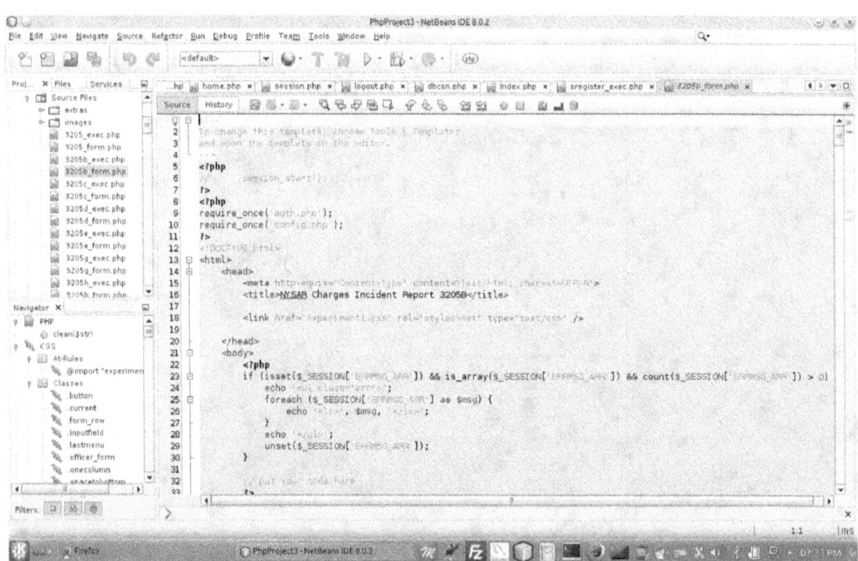

Figure 11: eCHIRPS Web Page Php Source Code (Partial)

Instead of calling the Sheriff Department looking for your loved one, wouldn't it be convenient to enter an email, phone, or social security number to search if the loved one is under arrest versus injured and in the hospital? Does the department have the ability to create there own virtual facilities? The ability to learn when, where, and the status of your case in the Criminal Justice System?

These last pages provided the information, availability, and skillsets of modern Pedagogy, Domain, and Learner Models desired to support an Artificial Intelligence Education Platform. Future educators should have the ability to write necessary source code, web page storyboards, and create databases. It was the classic story about when I was a kid we rode our bike uphill both ways in the rain. That story represents a different generation of students, a learning environment, adopting the new technology, and social expectations. Spelling errors were few, the potential re-write of research papers, three white-outs allowed, and all those pages! Negative reinforcement encouraging correct spelling and punctuation.

The slow introduction of Computer Technology influencing our daily interaction and work environment. What might you discover by having the parent of today describe their childhood and their learning environment? What might you learn or identify as new skillsets by having the students describe their experiences and comparing them over generations? What did any of Page 1 through Page 12 have to do with future learning environments? Writing is a method to enable, engage thought, compare, and expose the future (Webb, 2016).

While pursuing a Graduate Degree between 1988-1991 in Curriculum Development and Instruction, I composed this paper fulfilling a course requirement; <u>Teachers Beware: The Computer is After Your Job.</u> Ponder for a few moments, the instructor, and class response from up and rising educators to the title by itself! The concepts of "synthetic media" and "Fake News" did not exist in the ordinary course of engaging conversation. I encourage you to read the content in Figure 12. Today, to fulfill Figure 12 (the AI Tutor), and a part of the Learner Model (Figure 1), access to a database, a Facebook profile, or a specific Facebook Group is all that is needed to create the perfected personal tutor.

Last week's challenge: The plausible next-order impacts of synthetic media.

From: Anonymous Poster
Editor's note: We don't usually share community foresight posts without attribution. However, this one was so provocative that we've decided to break from our guidelines.

Amazon Prime Ed: Optimistic, circa 2030.
Synthetic media ushers in a new age of learning and certification. Tech leaders, already testing entry into education in the 20s, rush to create platforms offering synthetic versions of top educators and thought leaders, including those that have passed. This opens up opportunities to learn from the "best of the best" in any field and democratizes "world class" education. Early on, content is licensed as each professor (or estate) retains rights to the likeness and source material. New content developed by proprietary algorithms is owned by the content company however. Valuable data and fine-tuned interactions that "humanize" the experience are ultimately leveraged by synthetic content players to create hybrid professors, spinning the most effective aspects of "branded" synthetics off into private-label offerings. Read more community scenarios on algorithmic scoring.

Figure 12: Screenshot, Future Today Institute, Newsletter Issue:137

Kosinski et al. (2013) state, "We show that easily accessible digital records of behavior, Facebook Likes, can be used to automatically and accurately predict a range of highly sensitive personal attributes including sexual orientation, ethnicity, religious and political views, personality traits, intelligence, happiness, use of addictive substances, parental separation, age, and gender." Segalin et al. (2017) suggest personality characteristics such as extroversion and friendliness can be assessed based upon the Facebook profile. Personality is an essential characteristic of the Learner Model. Matz et al. (2017) go on to demonstrate how this information is used to manipulate individual and group behavior for positive and negative social implications during decision-making processes. A positive, this information contributes to enabling a precise, individualized education tutor for each student. It would respond to a student's strengths, weaknesses, preferences, interests, and preferred learning style.

Brunau (2020) created an overview of Computer-Based Games (CBG), Internet Video Games (IVG), and Collaborative Virtual Environments (CVE) describing the different system blueprints. Its content or the majority of its content are copied in the Chapter entitled Get-A-Way Games. It is entirely possible, a personal tutor and learning environment for each student using AI by 2030 could become a reality. It may be all our Public School Systems (K-12) should teach today is reading, writing, arithmetic, and social skills while moving toward "synthetic content players to create hybrid professors." Children could be grouped by their developmental age and grade level (K-2, 3-6, 7-9, 10-12, or the local school district standard grouping). The possibilities are infinite. For example, Hybrid home-school, alternating days in school, optional all on-line courses, or all at school courses (Academia vs. Trades Tracts) could potentially reduce class size and transportation demands.

Get-A-Way Games

This Chapter is a review, the development of, effects of, and potential vision for "software & technology" as "teacher" or "student" in the world of Artificial Intelligence (AI) copied from Brunau (2020). It was between 1988 and 1991 The Buffalo News (Figure 13, pg.16) and Pensacola News Journal published this Letter to the Editor. Charles Agel added the desktop computer photograph at the time of the original publication. Today, he designs and develops computer games. A modern cell phone has more power than the computer displayed in that photograph. Unfortunately, the responses from a past generation to those Letters were not saved. The predictions of these Letters were accurate regarding the future. It is because we can compare the past and the present over time that these Letters acquire value and enable advancement in Artificial Intelligence (AI). The future implications for Education or training are limitless for all students.

Computer Based Games (CBG), Internet Video Games (IVG), and Collaborative Virtual Environments (CVE) are all subject areas in Education and contribute data into the long term memory identified as Artificial Intelligence (AI). The National Center for Educational Statistics (NCES, updated May 2019) have started to assess competencies in an area termed Science Technology Engineering and Math (S.T.E.M.) or Technology and Engineering Literacy. Today is different because current assessment includes components collectively identified as *technology and society, design and systems or information and communication technology. "The National Assessment of Educational Progress (NAEP) Technology and Engineering Literacy (TEL)* assessment measures whether students are able to *apply technology and engineering skills to real-life situations. In the assessment framework, technology is defined as "any modification of the natural world done to fulfill human needs or desires," and engineering is defined as "a systematic and often iterative approach to designing objects, processes, and systems to meet human needs and wants."* Reaching into the future Baker et al.

(2019) authored <u>Educ-AI-tion Rebooted? Exploring the future of artificial intelligence in schools and colleges.</u>

The computer: Is it more than an intrusion in our lives?

Rampant computerism a threat to civilization

We accept the benefits that computer technology provides without question. We are in the early stages of computer dependency syndrome — the inability to function as a society or individual without a computer or the aid of a computer.

Today, the computer is our "significant other." We value and trust "computer output," hesitating to question it and giving it control over us. We make human-like attributes toward it, calling it "user-friendly" or a "thinking" machine.

During an unscheduled computer "shut down," losing our data, we feel loss, we are unable to proceed, engaging a bereavement cycle similar to what we experience when losing a loved one.

What about when the cashier is unable to make change? What if the register malfunctions? What about data-base management? Virtual-reality programs? Computer gambling?

CHRISTA E. WAITE
Boston

Figure 13: Buffalo News Version of Letter to Editor 1993

The National Center for Educational Statistics (NCES, updated May 2019) goes on to state: "Overall, 46 percent of 8th-grade students performed at or above the Proficient level on the National Assessment of Educational Progress Technology and

Engineering Literacy assessment in 2018. Some 49 percent of female students scored at or above the Proficient level, which was higher than the percentage for male students (44 percent). The percentage of students scoring at or above 'Proficient' was higher for Asian students (66 percent), White students (59 percent), and students of Two or more races (53 percent) than for Hispanic students (31 percent), American Indian/Alaska Native students (29 percent), and Black students (23 percent)." It's not the three R's protocol standard "readin, ritin, and rithmatic."

Barber (2001) and Yusuf (2010) show that performance of students exposed to Computer Assisted Instruction (CAI) either individually or cooperatively improved their performance in reading and biology course work. The National Center for Educational Statistics for Science performance (NCES, updated 2017) confirms this observation and states: "In 2015, the average 4th-grade science score (154) was higher than the score in 2009 (150). The average 8th-grade science score in 2015(154) was higher than the scores in both 2009 (150) and 2011 (152). The average 12th-grade science score in 2015 (150) was not measurably different from the score in 2009".

Can current social issues or concerns be re-learned, predicted or prevented with actions centered upon using Games (Computer Based Games, Internet Video Games, Collaborative Virtual Environments) and AI? The ability does exist to use technology to predict why children fail in school (Millman, 2018). Ten years ago, Wang, et al. (2009) inquired about implementing or using games to acquire learning objectives using CVE's. Then, five years later, Granic, Lobel, and Engels (2014) exclaimed they agree with many other mental health professionals that these games have enormous potential to teach new forms of thought, behavior, or even methods of intervention. They examined the positive effects of playing video games amid much of the research that is often examining the adverse effects. They categorize their games simultaneously occurring in a sliding scale within dual-dimensions from simple to complex and non-social to high social contextual environments. This (Granic, 2014) concept is displayed in Figure 14.

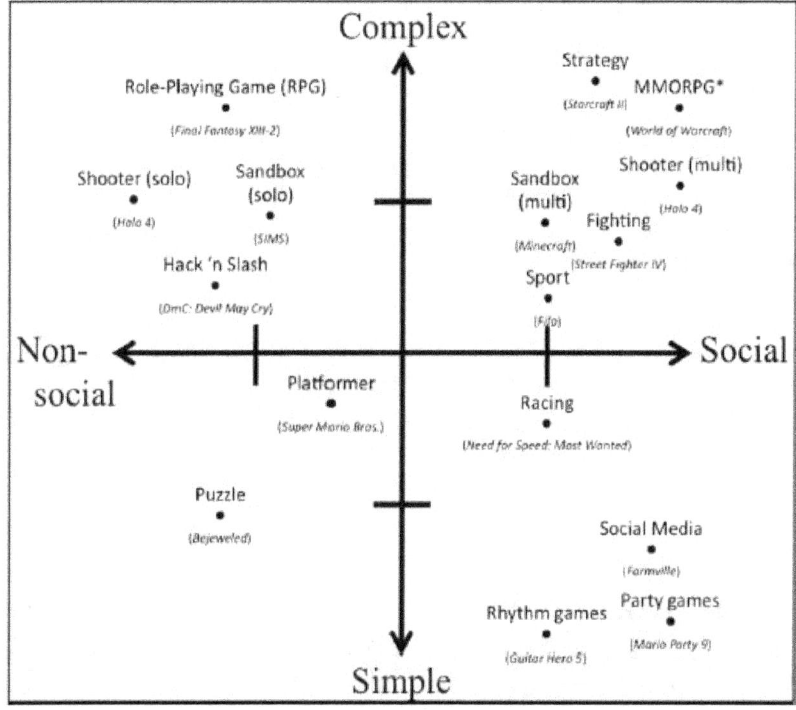

Figure 14: Conceptual Map of the Main Genres of Video Games. Screenshot from the Article Cited Granic, etal. (2014).

Meanwhile, developmental psychologists have been examining the benefits of play for children and allowing them to experiment with experiences, problem solving, and emotional consequences for decades. Piaget and Vygotsky both support the theories that elements of play foster social cognition. "Role-Play" is how children and adults can develop and understand power, authority, sadness, aggression, pain, or loss while moving through "simple to complex" and "non-social to high social" contextual game environments. Figure 15 describes the differences between Piaget and Vygotsky from McCleod (2018).

Figure 15: Screenshot Piaget and Vygotsky Theory from the URL diagram https://www.simplypsychology.org/vygotsky.html

	Piaget	Vygotsky
Sociocultural context	Little emphasis	Strong emphasis
Constructivism	Cognitive constructivist	Social constructivist
Stages	Strong emphasis on stages of development	No general stages of development proposed
Key processes in development & learning	Equilibration; schema; adaptation; assimilation; accommodation	Zone of proximal development; scaffolding; language/dialogue; tools of the culture
Role of language	Minimal – Language provides labels for children's experiences (egocentric speech)	Major – Language plays a powerful role in shaping thought
Teaching implications	Support children to explore their world and discover knowledge	Establish opportunities for children to learn with the teacher and more skilled peers

The Piaget and Vygotsky models fail to give credit to, show or allow the individual to move back toward "the self" or contribute and continue in building the self-concept (Rogers, 1959) after achieving reliance on other "knowledgeable's" or "tools" to learn tasks and skills. Simply stated, do you feel like a number, or do you have a sense of identity and worth? Equilibration? Bullying versus being bullied? Anxiety issues or concerns? Remember way back when there was the "fear of computers?"

Piaget asserts the self becomes more salient in the Concrete-operational (7-11 years of age) stage because it is where presumed awareness of others evolves or there is an awareness of others. The self includes a self-concept, including how you view yourself, how valuable you consider yourself in terms of self-esteem or self-worth, and what you strive for self-efficacy or your ideal self. Table 1 a summary of Rogers Self-Concept and Weiner's Theory of Attribution, while Table 2 presents the Locus of Control.

Carl Rogers Self-Concept	B. Weiner Attribution Theory
a self-concept including how you view yourself	Lack of Effort
how valuable you consider yourself in terms of self-esteem or self-worth	Lack of Ability
what you strive for self-efficacy or your ideal self	Ability/Effort
	Luck

Table 1: Carl Rogers (1959) and Weiner (2019) Summary

What do you attribution your performance to? Locus of Control		
	High (Perceived Ability)	**Low (Perceived Ability)**
Failure (Performance)	*Lack of Effort*	*Lack of Ability*
Success (Performance)	*Ability/Effort*	*Luck*

Table 2: Attribution Theory Working Table Locus of Control

A classic example to understand the Attribution Theory Working Table showing Locus of Control is the grade or game score someone might receive on a test or playing a video game. Weiner (1985) provides an expansive description of attribution and emotion and how this concept works in an application for those interested. A simple example, the statement the teacher gave me a "D" versus I made an "A" on the test. The "A" grade is where you might see yourself as having put a lot of effort and have a high degree of ability. Conversely, you might see yourself as just learning a game, and attribute the ability to play is not mastered, resulting in a low score. Attribution Theory is concerned with an individual's perceived Locus of Control. Locus of Control is an individual's belief system about their life experiences and the reasons a person assigns failure, blame, success, and credit.

Rogers (1959) founded the idea of self-concept and its components such as self-confidence, self-esteem or self-worth and ideal-self or more recently self-efficacy. Self-concept is how you see yourself. Self-efficacy and ideal self are beliefs about your ability or the person you strive to be. "Self-concept clarity (SCC) references a structural aspect of the self-concept: the extent to which self-beliefs are clearly and confidently defined, internally consistent, and stable" (Campbell. J.D. et al . 1996). Lee, C., et al. (2012) "found that compared with gamers with high self-concept clarity, gamers with low self-concept clarity spent more time playing video games" in college-age students. Ferla, J., Valcke, M., and Cai, Y. (2009) examined if academic self-efficacy and academic self-concept were two distinct components within the same domain of academics. They suggest, in regards to mathematics, a math self-concept does influence a student's math self-efficacy. Explicitly they state: "Academic self-concept is a better predictor (and mediator) for affective–motivational variables, while academic self-efficacy is the better predictor (and mediator) for academic achievement. " Stankov, etal. (2012) suggest confidence is a better predictor of academic success while noting self-efficacy, self-concept, and anxiety are components. Confidence is a distinct factor in the subjects Mathematics and English. The confidence we have in a given situation is the result of our self-concept, evidenced by attribution and our locus of control. It is our personal or subjective self-feedback about our formal education or learned experiences. What happens to Math confidence when the calculators are not allowed? The topic regarding the effects and influence of technology upon our self-perception and its effects can lead quickly and deeply into the weeds and hair-splitting terminology. It is not our purpose or intent to go to those depths into the topic but to provide a workable background to derive a foundation for decision making.

There are pictures, models, questions, and hypothetical scenarios for the future of formal Education. It appears a new constant is the application of mastery learning through CAI or Integrated Learning Systems (ILS) in the current system of Education. Student and Teacher are not mutually exclusive components of the Education System. While searching for more recent information providing descriptive information and data, this quote of Barber (2001) just flew off the page at me.

> They walk toward the classroom with determined yet excited expressions. Once the door opens, they scatter quickly to the perimeters of the room like leaves on a strong current of air. The moment they sit down they are busy with their own missions-fingers moving, machines humming, images flashing. Each child is actively engaged in reading, problem solving, analyzing, and learning… Sound like fiction? Not at all. This scenario is a description of an integrated learning system computer laboratory at a middle school in Northwest Florida.

Why does that quote fly off the page? Perhaps, it was such a contrast with Mr. Walter's classroom? A decade after Teachers Beware or the Buffalo News Letter? Could it be the mental echoes of "helicopter parenting," "smartphone addiction," and "snowflake" descriptions? Perhaps, it was the Rogerian "Man of Tomorrow" applied description?

> Person-centered education is a natural outgrowth of humanistic or Third Force psychology, which grew in large part in the 1970s as a reaction against the fact that behaviorist and Freudian approaches to therapy seem inadequate in dealing with the nature of *the higher human consciousness of man.* We can see the influence of the behaviorist in most of our schools today, as we watch teachers trying to condition students' behavior according to the academic goals of the teacher, frequently ignoring both the goals and actualization of the individual students. (Rogers, et al. 2014, pp.77)

Fortunately, it is election season and gathering the thoughts, and feelings of parents for their children's future education is relatively easy using screenshots of a candidate Facebook page. The School District, candidate, and respondent names have been removed using the software program Paint Shop Pro (white out brush tool not the liquid in a bottle)! Facebook is an Internet Open forum it seems appropriate to mask identities in this situation. The people were not asked if they wanted to be included in this text. These next screenshots display the candidate's question and a few sample responses from constituents appearing as contiguous paragraphs. Perhaps, most important, it is an example of being "person-centered" demonstrating a sense of empathy through inquiry, being genuine, and acknowledging each persons value with that "thumbs up." The "thumbs up" were removed from some of the

screenshots. The first view starts with "Dear Parents and Families,"
and the second "What a SWEET ice cream."

Dear   Parents and Families,

What are your hopes and dreams for your children's future???
I really want to know! Please reply and share.

Academically speaking, here is the gist of my
hopes and dreams for my children. I hope that they always have a
love of learning and are well-rounded individuals ready for the world.
I hope that they have excellent teachers and mentors and the
experiences, tools, and resources available to them in order to be
the best they can be in any path they choose.

Currently, that they have a safe and effective way
to get an education despite our current challenges as a country in
the middle of a pandemic. That their teachers will also be kept safe
so they can focus on what they do best: nurturing a love of learning.

Until that happens, it's really hard to focus on any future dreams.
This health crisis has changed my idea of the "future"... we just have
to try and get by week to week, day to day.

I hope they grow up with a love of reading. When I was a
little kid we had a reading program where you received points for
reading books and taking short quizzes on them. I still remember the
old programs like Reading Rainbow that encouraged me as well.
Regardless of what you want to accomplish in life a love of books
and reading can help you along the way.

I hope that my children can develop a love
for learning and their education and never want to stop learning. I
want them to be surrounded by those who will help me teach them
to serve others and value family, friends, and community. I want
them to attend schools that value and understand what it is to be a
kid; acknowledging that play and 'kid games' are a valuable part of
learning and growing. Instruction that is valuable and connected to
everyday life, not simply presented because that is what the "book"
says we do, is also important. I also want them to be afforded the
opportunity to learn about the rich history of this county so they can
understand the core values and principles that brought this nation
into being and what they can do to help continuously make it a great
nation. I fear this will disappear given current societal issues. I want
to see classrooms that foster all of these things without using the
term "FSA," which decreases a desire to enter the classroom on the
daily basis.

In a "perfect" classroom for my kids, it would be focused on learning skills that are appropriate for their age. We need to know that children are still children. Learning through play and social interactions are beneficial to their development. Give teachers an overall development criteria that each child needs to meet I order to progress to the next level instead of passing these ridiculous tests that everyone(teachers/students/parents) stress over. Do away with common core math. We all learned math perfectly fine growing up doing it the "old school" way so it needs to implemented back in. In the event that a child doesn't grasp that way, the teacher can then instruct that child.

Having a teenage student, I am looking for job readiness. I would love to have practical working skills to be able to apply the algebra and physics that we have learned in classroom. I would also love a split schedule combining virtual with brick and mortar. This would allow job scheduling to be more simplified as well as train him for online college.

My hopes for my children include them being able to flourish and seek out opportunity for education and career while showing their concern and care for community. Their mental and physical well-being are of the utmost importance to my husband and me. As a family, we strive to maintain values that are important to us; hard work, kindness, and health.

As parents it is our responsibility to provide our children with a solid foundation and offer them support to develop into the person they would like to be. All children should be afforded equal opportunities regardless of race, ethnicity, and economic standing. Public schools are one place where we can provide students and families with the tools they need to pave the way to a brighter future. Not all students will go on to college so it is important for us to expand vocational training programs and continue to foster positive relationships with businesses within our community. We have two teenage boys and my hope for them is that they will be able to graduate and leave Santa Rosa County School District prepared for the challenges of college or the workforce.

These Facebook screen shots display the comments and responses from an on-line inquiry and in-person event by the candidate. Observe the Likert type (strongly agree- 5 through strongly disagree-1) "thumbs, hearts and cares," and the totals. The quantity of comments, and shares. The different conditions either asking on-line what parents dream for their children's future or engaging with constituents directly. It is impossible to make any statistically significant statements concerning this observation of data but it seems to imply a preference for face-to-face social interactions to communicate (40 to 73 participants), and (14 to 7 shares) respectively. Alternatively, it could have been the ice cream on the hot day causing the in-person social event or the day of the week!

There are two other candidates running in this specific school district for the same position. The other candidates focus upon Ford's Model-T prescriptive for school safety in preparing students for employment. Only one candidate asking from the parent-student centered Rogerian approach and asking for their input. There is no doubt current technology in learning environments today is based on the principles of behavior modification. Rogers et al. (2014) go in depth to explore the person-centered approach to education and the beneficial outcomes that evolve from the process. It includes a method which can provide children, parents, adults, other friends with a sense of value and worth in a world dominated by anonymous coded data. Machines have not yet been programmed with the Psychology of Mind or Self-Replicating abilities. The evidence exist to demonstrate children, teenagers, even adults are able to acquire and learn almost any skill set, and have their own sense of right or wrong manipulated through the IoT. This leading to violence and a loss in their sense of self-concept, self-esteem, self-worth, or self-efficacy.

> Often a lack of real role models drives teenagers to draw back from initial reference persons and look for other guiding figures whose strength is expected to flow over them. The expectations from these new guiding figures match their own needs: To find ways out of experienced fear and helplessness. (Rogers, et al. 2014, pp. 138)

Behaviorism is most associated with the names Ivan Pavlov, J.B. Watson, and B.F. Skinner or research involving dogs, rats, and pigeons, respectively. The most basic form is what and how you train your dog to come when called or "sit" by command, hand signal, or using a "clicker." Treats and squirt bottles work wonders! It includes concepts like the stimulus, response, and reward. It is the "Magic Circle" (pp. 33) and inherently how, what, the medium, or the function of a computer and related tech equipment provide. For example, items like keyboards, mice, headsets, handsets, or monitors in the role(s) of stimulus and or response. It is also one of four Motivation Theories (2019) identified by the University of Buffalo Center for Educational Innovation (CEI). The web site provides a brief, compact, an easy and historical summation of theories in motivation categories identified as: Behavioral, Cognitive, Goals, and Expectancy-Value Models.

Expectancy-Value models motivation or the energy of our behavior. A car is usually a good example of this model. Expectancy-Value is an attempt to explain and understand if the car's performance (intrinsic) is more valuable or the appearance (extrinsic) to the owner and how that attribution process is determined or decided. It includes such things as ability, beliefs, intrinsic, extrinsic, locus of control, attribution, and expectations. Wigfield and Eccles (2000) examined the change in children's and adolescent components such as ability, expectancy, values, and the relationships related to their performance and choice of tasks. Figure 16 demonstrates the complexity of the Wigfield and Eccles Expectancy-Value Model. They are displaying significant interaction within a child or adolescent at the perception and interpretation boxes. It is not unreasonable to infer from this that perception and interpretation are life long actions. These perception-interpretation boxes are potentially where motivation is empowered.

Twenty years ago, Wigfield and Eccles (2000) initially created a questionnaire to assess five ability and task values in children in their contribution to the Expectancy-Value Model. These were identified as Ability Belief Items, Expectancy Items, Usefulness, Importance, and Interest Items. They used a questionnaire asked: "How good in math are you (Not at all good Very good), How well do you expect to do in math this year (Not at all well Very well), Some things that you learn in school help you do things better outside of class, that is, they are useful. For example, learning about plants might help you grow a garden. In general, how useful is what you learn in math (Not at all useful very useful). The children's ability-related beliefs and values become more negative in many ways as they get older, at least through early adolescence. Children believe they are less competent in many activities and often value those activities less." Hypothetically, you could create your questions and just remove and replace them as desired using the previous examples.

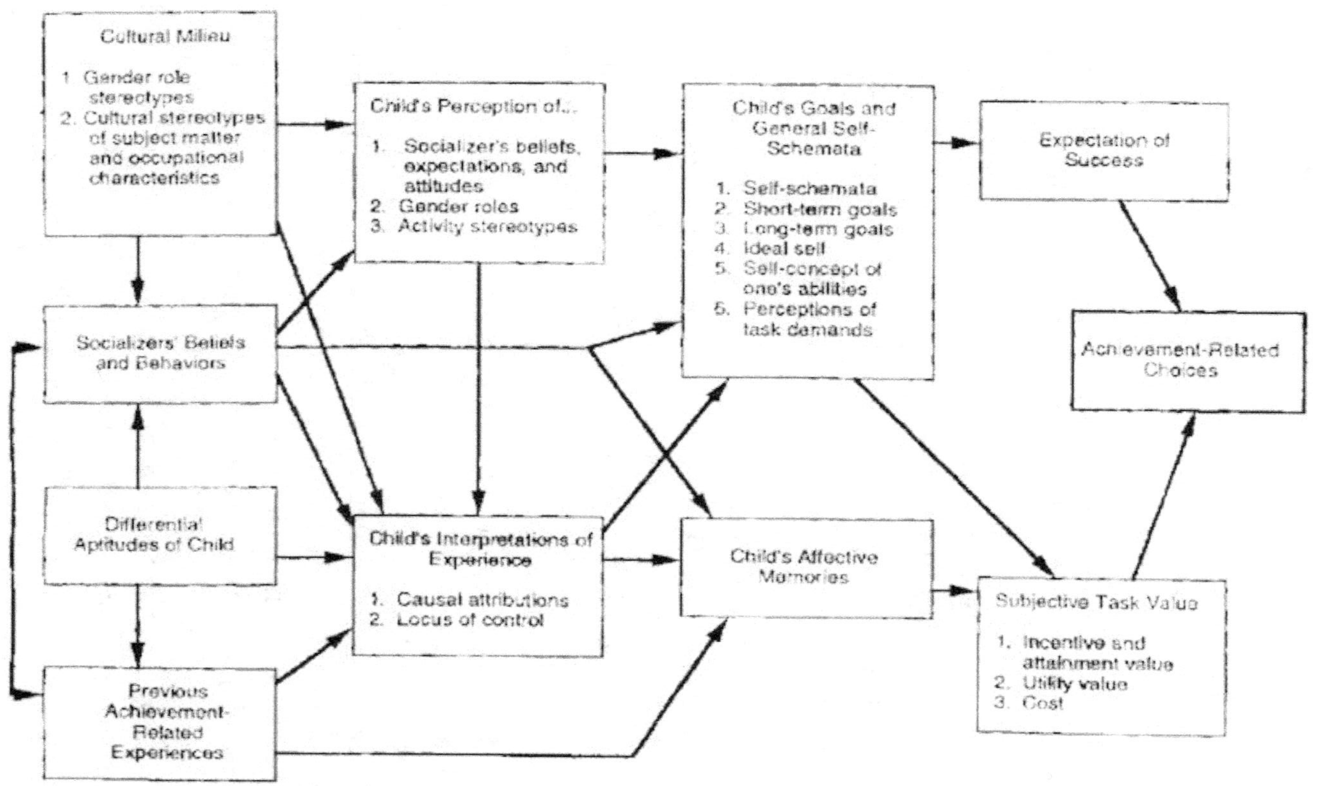

Figure 16: Screen shot from Wigfield, Eccles and colleagues (2000) expectancy-value model of achievement motivation

30

Recently, Barron and Hulleman (2014) contribute to the Expectancy-Value Models by adding a component identified as "Cost." Expectancy-Value models of motivation stand out because of their ability to incorporate a variety of perspectives, identifying elements of what motivates an individual, and explain achievement-related behaviors. The Expectancy-Value models have centered on the importance of two components in promoting overall motivation: having an expectancy and value. Perhaps, might "Cost" be considered a method to account for Locus of Control and make the model more inclusive?

Citing Barron and Hulleman (2014) in their description toward understanding the idea of cost, "consider the following three students enrolled in a calculus course. Math is a challenging subject for Rory, but by putting in extra effort and adopting the appropriate study strategies, he has been able to perform well in prior coursework. However, he finally met his match with calculus. Even with additional effort, he is unable to understand the material. As a result, he lacks confidence that he will do well, and his motivation for calculus has decreased. In contrast, math is an easy subject for Jeff. He's always scored at the top of his class and continues to do well in calculus. But this year, his motivation also has substantially decreased. Jeff struggles to see the utility of learning calculus and how he'll use it in the future. Finally, there is Jessica, who excels in math and finds it to be one of her favorite classes. She is also interested in several science careers that use calculus. However, due to an ambitious academic and extracurricular schedule, she is struggling to find enough time to complete her school work. In particular, her grades in math have suffered. She knows she could do it; she just cannot find the time, She too, now admits, her motivation in math is not what it used to be."

The simple way to sum these parts is to say Rory lacks confidence-expectancy, and Jeff is conflicted by value. Jessica, in contrast, has confidence-expectancy and value, but a lack of available time, extracurricular activities, or academic ambition are a "cost" or reason for her interpreted lesser motivation. Or, perhaps a restatement of Locus of Control to make it inclusive in the model. The creation of an Expectancy-Value-Cost Model allows for accountability for many of the parts involved with motivation. What is the motivation for violence?

Khenissi et al., (2016) expand on the numerous other assessment tools available, different complexities and relationships, the concerns and issues regarding variations of the definition, testing, validity, and reliability aspects, and consensus within the field of software game development specialist and education specialist. They agreed to use the Felder-Silverman (Table 1) criteria to categorize these learning styles to be the best fit model for the course of their research investigation. The Felder-Silverman Learning Style Model (FSLSM) identify preferences such as: Sensing-Intuitive, Visual-Verbal, Active-Reflective, and Sequential-Global within the game genre. They went on to describe and define Game Genre Categories, and they are displayed in Table 2. They found in their study. Sequential learners prefer Puzzle Games and those with a Sensing learning style preference for Casual Games. They suggest that presenting the learner with the preferred game genre matched with learning style has the potential to optimize the learner's experience and therefore lead to success.

What about God Games and Simulation Games' learning styles? Personality type? Or Personality style? Why not use the Myers-Briggs Inventory or Kiersey Temperament Inventory instead of FSLSM? Are God Games or Simulation Games a Learning Style question, or is a Personality Type involved? A Personality requiring an assessment? A Google search of Learning Style versus Personality Style, or Personality Type will provide a lot of studies and information relevant to legislators, parents, educators, and game developers. For example, just for fun, identify your learning style while exploring Human Metrics at this URL accessed on 13 January 2019: http://www.humanmetrics.com/personality/learning-styles Just remember where this data goes in the end!

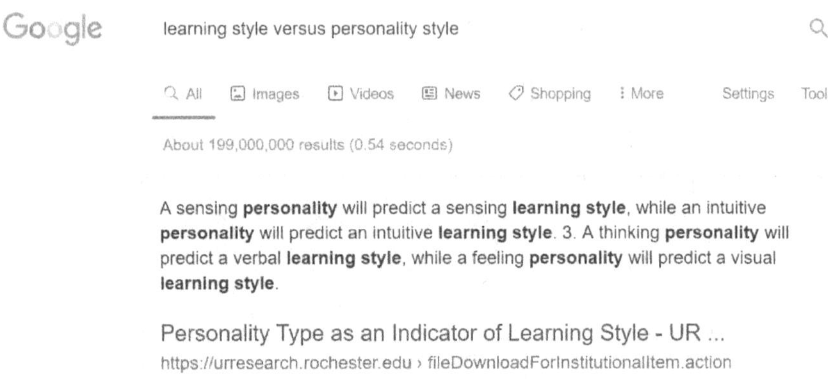

Figure 17: Google Search Learning Style versus Personality Style

Jenna Melvin's paper titled <u>Personality Type as an Indicator of Learning Style</u> is shown in the Search result of Figure 17. A summary image from Melvin's paper is presented in Figure 18. The Melvin Study and Khenissi Study vary slightly. She used the Jung Typology Test to determine Personality Type. She did not indicate if she was assessing the CBG, IVG, or CVE learning environment medium at the time of her study. However, it did look at the personality type of the "presenter" of the materials. Khenissi et al, looked at the "medium" for presenting the materials (CBG, IVG, CVE).

Melvin and Khenissi are both aware of FSLSM even though their results vary slightly. They were examining different things in one case, a "person" and the other a "game" as a source for "learning materials." How do you assess the "personality style" of a "game?" Do you have to determine the personality of the learner instead? Regardless, we now have "Game Genre" categories. Is "game genre" the new alternative personality style?

Wang, etal. (2009) perform an extensive review examining collaborative learning, characteristics, models, and their taxonomy. They suggest games with the highest educational value are those developed for a specific subject, and they come with the highest cost to produce. For example, Military Flight Simulation Training this offered by Textron (URL https://www.trusimulation.com/military-simulation-services). *It is presumed in this paper that high education value, specific subject, and high development cost is the equivalent of assessing the Best Selling Games for 2019* (see Table 3) revealed by a Google Search. For example, the Call of Duty:

Modern Warfare website "available jobs," Veterans can apply for a position as a Subject Matter Expert (SME). Official "game players" can apply with Activision, where experience is a pre-requisite. These two sites and services (Textron and Activision) were both accessed on 19 December 2019. What Khenissi Game Genre would you assign to these examples from Textron and Activision? What about Webb's (2019) Top 10 Selling Video Games each listed?

Granic et al (2014) pursued "the research on the benefits of playing video games while focusing on four main domains: cognitive (e.g., attention), motivational (e.g., resilience in the face of failure), emotional (e.g., mood-management), and social (e.g., prosocial behavior) benefits."

Figure 18: Jenna Melvin's Screenshot from the Paper titled Personality Type as an Indicator of Learning Style Summaries.

Personality Type[1]	Learning Style[2]
Extravert	**Active**
*I like getting my energy from active involvement in events *I often understand a problem better when I can talk out loud about it and hear what others have to say	*Active learners tend to retain and understand information best by doing something active with it--discussing or applying it or explaining it to others
Introvert	**Reflective**
*I take time to reflect so that I have a clear idea of what I'll be doing when I decide to act *I often prefer doing things alone or with one or two people I feel comfortable with	*Reflective learners prefer to think about it quietly first *Prefer working alone
Sensing	**Sensing**
*I notice facts and I remember details that are important to me. *I like to see the practical use of things and learn best when I see how to use what I'm learning.	*Sensing learners tend to like learning facts and be patient with details *Sensors tend to be more practical and careful
Intuitive	**Intuitive**
*I'm interested in new things and what might be possible *I like to work with symbols or abstract theories	*Intuitive learners often prefer discovering possibilities and relationships *Often more comfortable with abstractions and mathematical formulations
Thinking	**Verbal**
*I like to find the basic truth or principle to be applied *I look for logical explanations	*Verbal learners get more out of words--written and spoken explanations
Feeling	**Visual**
*I believe I can make the best decisions by weighing what people care about and the points-of-view of persons involved in a situation	*Visual learners remember best what they see--pictures, diagrams, flow charts, time lines, films, and demonstrations
Judging	**Sequential**
*I seem to prefer a planned or orderly way of life and like to have things settled and organized	*Sequential learners tend to follow logical stepwise paths in finding solutions
Perceiving	**Global**
*I seem to prefer a flexible and spontaneous way of life, and I like to understand and adapt to the world rather than organize it	*Global learners tend to learn in large jumps, absorbing material almost randomly without seeing connections, and then suddenly "getting it."

---

[1] Information taken from *MBTI basics* (The Myers & Briggs Foundation)
[2] Information taken from *Learning styles and strategies* (Soloman & Felder)

Table 1: Felder-Silverman Learning Style Model Summary
Khenissi, Essalmi, Jemni, etal., (2016)

Style	Characteristic
Active/Reflective	Active learners like to try things out and interact with the materials. Reflective learners like to think about thinks on their own and reflect upon the material.
Sequential/Global	Sequential learners like to learn step by step, sequentially, simple to complex. Global learners prefer a holistic presentation, they look at the whole, they are interested in broad overviews and able to solve complex unaware of how they reached their solution to the problem.
Sensing/Intuitive	Sensing learners follow facts and use standard methods, patient with details and dislike surprises or unexpected effects. Intuitive learners prefer to discover relationships, creative and innovative, dislike repetition and bored by details.
Visual/Verbal	Visual learners prefer pictures, diagrams, flow charts, frequently forget words. Verbal learners remember much of what they hear and more of what they hear and say. Learn best by explaining things to others.

Table 2: Khenissi etal Game Genre Characterization (2016)

M.A. Khenissi, etal Game Genre Categories	
Genre	**Description**
Puzzle Games	Puzzle games do not have a player-conflict component. They have no story line they are just presented like a jigsaw puzzle and require a procedural step by step process to complete or "win."
God Games	They have no preset "win" condition. The players are presented a set of tools and a global view of the environment. They choose their own path.
Casual Games	These are simple and easy to learn. They do not require any previous knowledge or special skills to "win."
Simulation Games	These games depend on imagination and creativity to manage communities or do things that are not possible in the real world to "win".

Pleasant and Ritzhaupt (2013) performed a book review of <u>Video Games and Learning: Teaching and Participatory Culture in the Digital Age</u> by Kurt Squire. They state: "Squire believes that play enables the intellectual and social growth of the participant over the long term and *permeates* into his or her learning repertoire. He believes that content, overlapping goals, continuous problem solving, social interactions and gaming cultures are critical aspects of learning through games...good games must be a collaborative work of designers and educators, be entertaining and academically accurate, be fun and insightful, be sophisticated using proven design techniques, provide social networks, group interactions, pique interests, and inspire creativity".

Table 3: Webb's (2019) Top 10 Selling Video Games

Name of Game	Manufacturer
10. Anthem	BioWare/Electronic Arts (EA)
9. Star Wars Jedi: Fallen Order	EA/Respawn Entertainment
8. Super Smash Bros. Ultimate	Nintendo
7. Tom Clancy's The Division 2	Ubisoft
6. Kingdom Hearts 3	Square Enix
5. Mortal Kombat 11	Warner Bros. Interactive
4. Borderlands 3	Take 2 Interactive
3. Madden NFL 20	Electronic Arts
2. NBA 2K20	Take 2 Interactive
1. Call of Duty: Modern Warfare	Activision

Plass, Homer, and Kinzer (2015) provide an extensive and comprehensive overview of the Foundations of Game Based Learning. They state: "In this article, we aim to provide a comprehensive theory-based approach to games and learning that incorporates multiple views of learning and foundations of game design. To that end, we first discuss the definitions of game based learning, and the theoretical models that can describe learning with games. We then describe the design elements of games that facilitate learning. Last, we summarize how the design of these game elements is based on cognitive, motivational, affective, and socio-cultural foundations." Figure 19 is their "Behavior Modification" Magic Circle Model of Game Based Learning and Figure 20 is the Integrated Design Framework for Game Based and

Playful Learning. They suggest the amount of time spent playing games *varies by gender*, 7-10 hours per week, by the *type of game*, but there are *no apparent differences* in learning or motivation.

Gaming, databases, data collection, and technology under the "Artificial Intelligence" (AI) umbrella contribute to and enable us to "predict" future behavior and "react" but cannot use "wise" judgment. The assessment confirms we can use "technology" but are we failing to assess our *actual* ability to perform the task itself?

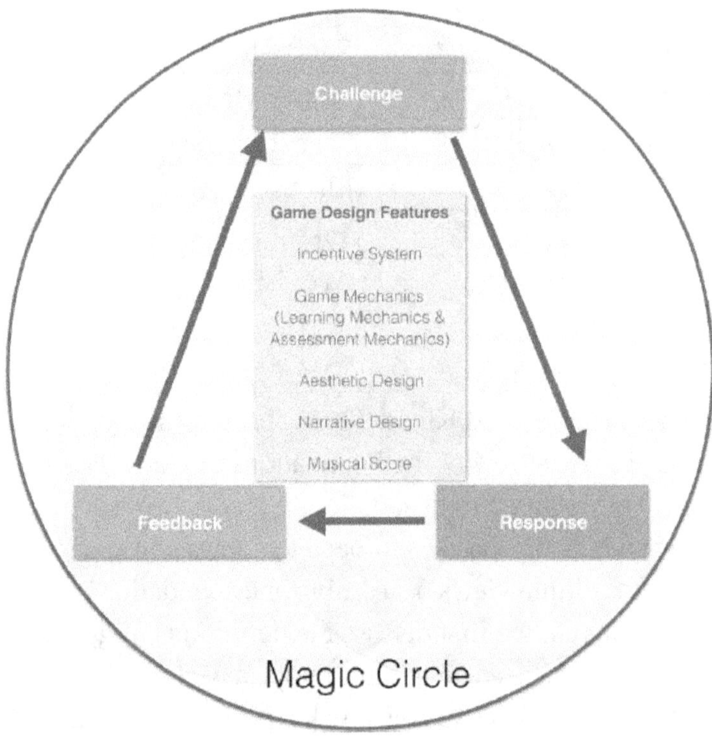

Figure 19: Plass, Homer, Kinzer (2015) Magic Circle Model of Game Based Learning, pp 262

Does this difference in actual ability, what we can do or are not able to do, with or without technology, contribute to violent behavior or bullying behavior? Alternatively, is it a demonstration of anxiety or frustration contributing to violent behavior or bullying behavior? Concept of our self? In general, what seems not to be determined is the question, are we creating an illusion concerning subject areas, tasks, or desired skills we can perform? Is this false attribution contributing to our increase in violence? Reduced confidence in our actual abilities leading to and contributing to frustration and violence?

The game of Pong (created by Nolan Bushnell of children's favorite Chuck-E-Cheese Pizza fame) through Activision's Call Of Duty demonstrates the advances in technology used with computer based games over the past fifty years. It also shows the comprehensive and well developed blueprints of our own "being" available to create games that are enabling us to learn any subject area, task, or desired skill. It is not a simple "cause and effect" relationship; instead, it is a complicated and interactive relationship involved between the source and learner.

It is not difficult to perform a search of all types of games. There are games for education, games for academics, games for students in their school districts, there are all types of technology "Internet of Things" based methods of learning. The model and criteria for teacher certification, education, and learning need to be changed to coincide with the needs of the future. Should future teacher certification require an additional qualification in Counseling or Mental Health, or an increase in required course work concentrated in classic trade occupations? Is everyone destined for or even suited for College? It is obvious this is a complex issue, but the tools, building blocks, and environment still support the means and methods to acquire a skill set for the future.

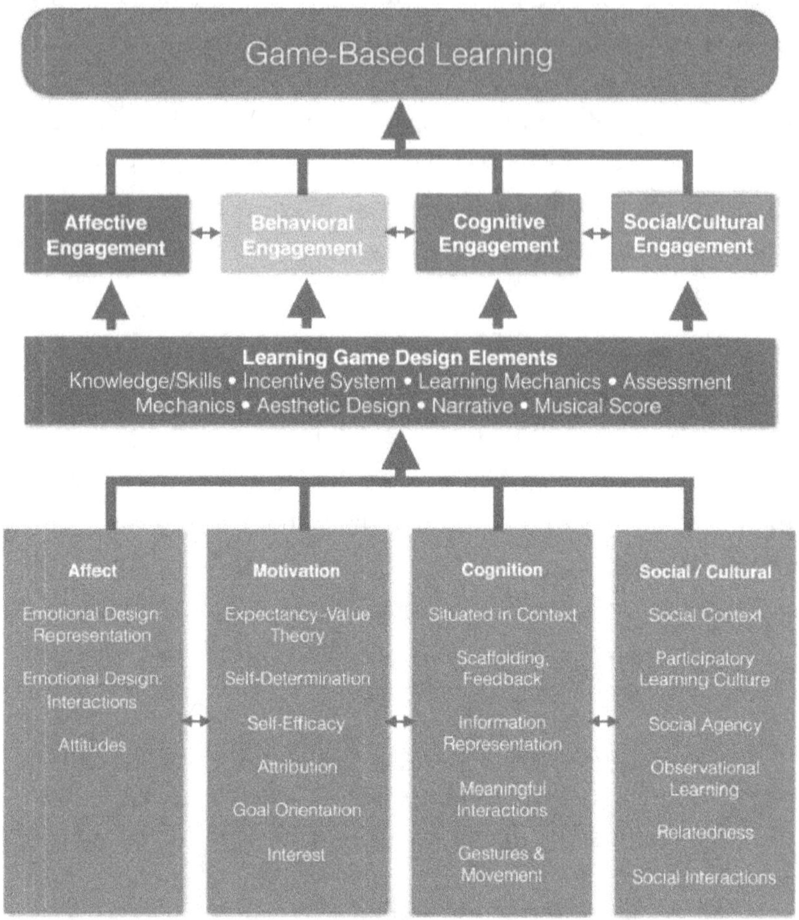

Figure 20: Plass, Homer, Kinzer (2015) Integrated Design Framework for Game Based and Playful Learning pp 263

We have the "blue print" to create any computer based game desired. We have touched on "Sequential-Global" learners. The materials and software are available to do an enormous amount of beneficial things with technology.

Quote Other Brunau Opinion Essays

This section of this opinion essay includes quotes from Bitcoin (BTC): The Art of Artificial Intelligence Warfare (Brunau, 2018).

It seems an irony where a Letter to the Editor publication (at the start of this book) would lead to almost 30 years later! It certainly would have been so much easier to complete this writing brief with the assistance of modern technology. I suspect the research performed then would likely be lost on some floppy, CD or USB over the years versus being kept on paper. It must be noted the following pages may be repetitive as the collection of papers is finally being manually entered into the digital world. This composite of research might have been the required "book report," one of those research article assigned for the three day weekend in college, an article submitted to the Journal of Computer Assisted Instruction or a presentation accounting for the graduate course grade in analysis in teaching methods. "Google It" was not an option because it did not exist! All sources used and available will be cited in the References section. A couple research papers examined predicting personality type of a hacker and Maslow's Stock picking theory. Admittedly, after this amount of time, even this research is missing a couple pages and represent what is left in "hard copy" and represents a lot of under-graduate and graduate work. There may be some "figures and diagrams" missing after all these years. Dragon speak does not work with Linux…..probably still have papers somewhere with the limited use of "white out" being allowed! There are microscope, hand drawings of muscle and vascular systems from the very early 80's! Who knows maybe the "Fires of Alexandria in Egypt" were due to a failure of technology rather than an actual burning of documents stored.

<u>Teachers Beware; The Computer is After Your Job.</u> This paper provides a brief historical development of the computer and likely familiar reading. It provides information concerning the "forefathers" of computers, the "mechanical" changes and developments, the areas of computer application, criterion used for determining its application, its effect on the skilled labor force, possible limitations, advantages and disadvantages in corporate America. It also poses questions for the future of education and administrative uses. Also, questions pertaining to the effect and affect it may have on the human entity of the future. It looks at the current traditional school curriculum. Finally, it attempts to alter how we view the computer in such a positive light.

Computers are not necessarily new. They can be traced back to the abacus and the counting machines of Pascal and Leibniz. More recently, during the mid-nineteenth century engineers such as Babbage, Jaquard, and Hollerith were making use of primitive computers in the work place. Babbage is responsible for the development of calculation for his machines and the tools required to build them. Jaquard developed systems for punching cards with instructions so that a loom could reproduce a design or a portrait. Hollerith combined the card-reading machine with a tabulator to produce the world's first mechanical data processor. Hollerith also combined traits found repeatedly in the history of the computer (i.e., how to use technology to solve certain types of problems and a desire to see commercial applications of his ideas). Today, Hollerith's company is a dominate force in the computer industry commonly referred to as the International Business Machines Corporation, or IBM.

The computer originated in the laboratory, and it was primarily used in scientific and military applications. The first major funds towards development came from the defense budget. That is where the first decimal computer was developed, ENIAC (Electronic Numerical Integrator and Computer), a product of World War II ballistic research. However, the ENIAC project was too late to be used as an influencing factor in the war. Consequently, ENIAC was applied to the Los Alamos calculations for the development of the hydrogen bomb.

This increased potential uses of computers resulted in changes of the computers mechanics. The first major breakthrough came when mechanical tape replaced vacuum tubes for storing memory. Another major accomplishment was the Whirlwind Project which produced the first "real time" computer. It was a system that combined several computers and devices to coordinate information. It was also the first computer to use a magnetic core memory and interactive monitors. It could be used for assembly lines and air traffic control. It also appears to be the "parent" of the mini/micro computer of the 1990'. Another breakthrough occurred with the advent of the transistor (1947) and the integrated circuit (1959) which lead to the "solid state or semi-conductor devices." Finally, the most recent advancement came in the form of the general purpose logic chip (1971). By combining the "memory" with the logic chip, the micro-computer can be used in any machine that manipulates information (i.e., thermostats and home appliances). Its has also made possible increased memory storage at low cost as well as accelerated the development of robotics.

Currently, (up to 1988) the Cray-2 has the world's largest internal memory capacity (2 billion bytes),

240,000 computer chips are used. It is 40 to 50,000 time faster than a personal computer (i.e., Apple II, IBM PC) in speed alone. Livermore stated: "What took a year in 1952 we can now do in a second." Today, it appears that the computer is basically a capital-intensive, labor saving device. It rationalizes task completion. It works well in the current corporate structure, which is based on centralized decision making. It also adapts functionally to the needs of the new entrepreneurial corporations. Computer networks enable a company or a group to transcend the conventional limits of time and space.

On the other hand, by their nature and formidable capability computers are changing the workplace. A great deal of labor is now organized to work with the computer rather than direct it. As a result, workers are not only losing their control over their work, they are also losing control over their work, they are also losing their understanding of it. As computers control more aspects of work, the gap between knowledge workers, who control the technology, and line workers, who are its custodians, will become wider. In the process, a number of skilled jobs will simply disappear, as intelligent machines become capable of performing more tasks with competence that exceeds that of human workers. Currently, the primary question being asked, how much risk is involved in a specific task? (i.e., toxic waste, weather conditions, working conditions). Another factor used is the speed and accuracy (i.e., spot welding). During the initial implementation of robotics in the early 1980's and average of 2.2 jobs were eliminated. It is estimated for every 2.5 jobs lost to robotics only four-fifths of a new job is created. It is also estimated the U.S. will lose up to 200,000 manufacturing jobs to robotics. The justification is found in the decreased costs of extra pay for hazardous and unpleasant working conditions, as well as of workplace insurance and disability, are the obvious benefit of this sector.

The savings for corporate America are not immediate. Granted, in work situations where precision and accuracy are the basis of cost-profit ratios, computerized equipment can increase profits but only if it is introduced with adequate knowledge and training for those who maintain and use it. Without appropriate training workers who use the computer unintentionally cause it to break down. Repeatedly, companies overestimate the transition from blue collar to metal collar as being easy, and underestimate the training cost involved.

Another problem with automation is worker resistance, unintentional and intentional. The Campbell Soup Company made a decision to computerize the "master soup-taster's job". The hidden aspects of job competence are consistently the most difficult to teach a machine. These are often highly variable and unquantifiable: they involve experience, trial and error, and sense, touch or knack. It took the soup-taster and a programmer more than three months to map out the job so that it could be programmed.

The most threatened group of workers are managers. A good deal of what managers do is gather information informally in ways which resist documentation. This makes it unlikely that electronic management systems will ever attain the capabilities of human managers.

Through this brief 150 year history of computer development certain questions can be raised about the future of education and its administrative practices. It appears that advances in the computer technology are progressing more rapidly than the human entity can keep up with. Reflecting upon various class presentations it seems possible that the traditional job of being a teacher is nearing its end. That is to say, the "traditional" subject matter (math, science, English and social studies) is subject to be replaced with 'non-traditional" subject matter (computer programming, interpersonal skills training and group therapy). A question which may support this is, what is the correlation between high tech industries and the number of "team building" or "quality circles" training programs offered? It is also possible, computerization has provided the extra time to conduct such training seminars. Interpersonal skills training could be introduced due to reduced time in social interaction. If television is correlated with causing desensitization of some human feelings or emotions (crime, war, violence programs) it is possible that a high degree of computer interaction among human entities may result in an overall reduction of feelings and emotions. It is normal for an individual to imitate or acquire the behaviors and attributes of a "significant other" who enters their life? What are the qualities which cause someone to become a significant other in a persons life? Are these qualities found in a computer?

Then, somewhere between 1991-1994 came <u>Computers in Education: Their Influence upon Academic and Computer Self-Efficacy</u> where the Abstract states the purpose of this study was to determine whether a computer was able to influence academic and computer self-efficacy. A significant difference in academic self-efficacy was identified between those who had a computer and did not have a computer, $F (1, 52) = 4.47$, $p <. .03$). A significant difference was identified among those who did not have a computer when the degrees of human-computer interaction varied, $F(3,56) = 6.3$, p

< .001). Computer self-efficacy accounted for 27% of the variance in academic self-efficacy, F (1, 64) = 5.096, p < .02). Computer anxiety accounted for 50% of the variance in computer self-efficacy, F (1, 64) = 21.312, p < .000). A total of 122 subjects participated in this study. The current academic performance appraisal methods are introduced and questioned. The possibility of Computer Dependency is introduced. Computer Dependency is the inability to perform some task without a computer r the aid of a computer. (The remainder of this section describes in more detail the actual study with more details if interested. If you are not interested just skip and go on to the next Chapter).

Introduction Does a computer influence the number of academic courses subjects believe they are able to pass? Is there a relationship between the number of courses they believe they can pass using a computer and the belief in their ability to pass these courses? Is there a relationship between academic efficacy, computer efficacy, and computer anxiety? Does the computer influence computer efficacy?

The benefits of using computers in education are influenced by the attitudes that are held toward them by the user, such as computer anxiety. Woodrow (1991) describes computer anxiety as a lack of confidence or having negative feelings about one's ability to use the computer. Mevarech and BenArtzi (1986) found that computers can improve academic achievement; and influence an aspect of the self-concept, self-esteem (Robetson, Ladewig, Strickland, and Boschung, 1987; Rosenberg and Turner, 1981). Computers have also been associated with negative physiological side effects, such as Carpal

Tunnel Syndrome, and by the radiation emissions given off from the visual display terminals (Kusack, 1990; and Morgan, 1990). In the past, researchers have explained the difference in their results concerning academic self-efficacy and computer self-efficacy to such factors as gender, interest, ethnicity, and socioeconomic status (Hackett, Betz, Casas, and Rocha-Singh, 1992; Muira, 1986; 1987).

Self-efficacy theory suggest that self-efficacy expectancies have a strong effect upon behavior and behavior change (Hill, Smith, Mann, 1987; Sherer and Adams, 1983). Schunk (1991) describes self-efficacy as an individual's judgment of his or her ability to perform a given task. There are other forms of efficacy that are more specific, such as academic and computer self-efficacy (Hackett, Betz, Casas, and Rocha-Singh, 1992; Owen and Froman, 1988). Academic and computer self-efficacy are an individual's belief in his or her ability to perform the expected tasks of an academic course; and a belief in his or her ability to use a computer respectively (Hill, Smith, Mann; 1987; Miura, 1986, 1987;, Owen and Froman, 1988; and Murphy, 1988). Self-efficacy is a factor of the self-concept that is influential in explaining students' learning and performance (Schunk, D.H., 1989;1991).

The literature states that having or using a computer can influence the self-esteem of a student (Robertson, Ladewig, Strickland and Boschung, 1987). Because self-efficacy is a part of the selfconcept, it also might be influenced by human-computer interaction. The identification of more specific types of self-efficacy, such as computer self-efficacy and academic self-efficacy, suggest it is also true that having or using a computer might influence these specific forms of self-efficacy (Miura, 1986; 1987; Owen and Froman, 1988;

and Murphy, 1988). Since computer anxiety can influence humancomputer interaction it may play a role in computer efficacy (Woodrow, 1991), Self-efficacy appears to be an additive concept; the more tasks or behaviors one believes he or she is able to perform, the higher one is in total self-efficacy (McGowan, 1986; Sherer and Adams, 1983; and Shunk, 1987, 1989, 1991).

Self-efficacy is the belief that one can successfully perform a task or behavior. Academic selfefficacy is the belief one can pass an academic course; and computer self-efficacy is the belief one can use a computer. Computer anxiety is a lack of confidence or negative feelings about one's ability to use the computer. Academic self-efficacy in this study is the amount of academic courses subjects believed they could pass or how confident they were in their ability to pass. Computer self-efficacy in this study refers to the subjects belief or confidence in their ability to use a computer.

Method Study 1 was to determine whether a computer influenced the number of college academic courses subjects believed they could pass. Fifty-six subjects were asked to complete a questionnaire, Form A or Form B, containing a 16 item academic course check list. Form A directed subjects to place a check mark before each subject that they believed they would be able to pass using a computer. Both Forms A and B asked the respondents if they had a computer.

Study 2 was to assess additional information toward explaining the results that had been identified in the first study. Sixty-six subjects were asked to complete a questionnaire containing the same 16 item academic check list used in the first study. Form C informed subjects that the following courses made heavy use of computers and directed them to place a check mark before each course they believed they would be able to pass. Form D informed subjects that the following courses were Computer Assisted Instruction (CAI) and directed them to place a check mark before each course they believed they would be able to pass. Form C and Form D also asked the respondents if they had a computer.

The C and D Forms included a Likert type scale to assess information concerning: 1) a possible relationship between the number of academic courses subjects believed they could pass using a computer and the belief they held about their ability to pass the courses, 2) a possible relationship between academic efficacy, computer efficacy, and computer anxiety, and 3) whether a computer influenced computer efficacy.

The Likert type scale asked subjects to strongly disagree (1), or strongly agree (5), with the following statements: 1) I am confident about my ability to pass, 2) I am confident about my ability to use a computer, and 3) Computers make me nervous. The academic, computer, and anxiety Likert scale responses were correlated with the dependent variable "items checkd," and with one another. Regression procedures were also used.

Study 3 was to recreate the main effect found during the first study by creating two separate 1 x 4 designs. The third study evolved due to the main effect found during the first study and the lack of an expected interaction after the inclusion of data from the second study.

In the first study, a significant main effect in the dependent variable "items checked" was identified between subjects who indicated they had a computer

and those who indicated they did not have a computer.
The second study was added to assess additional
information toward explaining this main effect.
However, the main effect of the first study was not
significant after including the data from the second
study. Instead, a significant main effect was identified
for Form A, B, C, and D; the varying degrees of human-
computer interaction evolving from the data added by
the second study.

The third study reinstated the findings of the first study
by creating two separate 1 x 4 designs.

Subjects were categorized as to whether they did not
have a computer as well as by Form A, B, C, or D, or
whether they did have a computer as well as by Form A,
B, C, or D. There were 60 subjects assigned to the "did
not have a computer" group, and 62 subjects assigned to
the "have a computer" group in the third in the third
study.

Overall, a total of 122 subjects were asked to complete
a questionnaire containing a 16 item academic course
check list with each Form varying in the degrees of
human-computer interaction. Respondents were
categorized by: (1) Form A, B, C or D, and (2) whether
they had or did not have a computer. The questionnaires
also asked for a subject's age and sex.

Subjects were a random sample of 122 undergraduate
students from Erie Community College and the
Canisius College of Buffalo. There were 57 females and
65 males with a mean age of 21.9.

Results where the overall purpose of the study was to
determine whether: (1) a computer influenced the
number of college academic courses subjects believed

they could pass, (2) a relationship existed between the number of courses they believed they could pass using a computer and a belief in their ability to pass, (3) a relationship existed between academic efficacy, computer efficacy, and computer anxiety, and (4) having a computer influenced computer efficacy. Because there has not been any research conducted addressing these issues as a collective unit toward explaining the differences in academic or computer self-efficacy among subjects and because research has been limited in whether the computer is able to effect any other aspect of the self-concept, this study provides additional information for the related fields of education and psychology.

The alpha level was preset at $p < .05$. Table 1 (not included in this manual to digital recreation) shows the cell size, means and standard deviations for each of the groups that participated in the study.

Study 1 does a computer influence the number of college academic courses subjects believed they would be able to pass? The results of the first study suggest that the answer is "yes." The 2 x 2 (Computer * Form) ANOVA revealed a significant main effect between subjects who indicated they had a computer and those who indicated they did not have a computer, $F(1, 52) = 4.47$, $p < .03$), with the number of "items checked" as the dependent variable.

Study 2 is there a relationship between the number of courses subjects believed they could pass using a computer and a belief in their ability to pass? Is there a relationship between academic efficacy, computer efficacy, and computer anxiety? Does a computer influence computer efficacy? The results of the second study suggest that the answer to these questions is "yes." In the second study, a correlation of. .496 was found for the dependent variable "items checked" and the Likert scale items assessing academic efficacy; a .272 between academic efficacy (Likert scale) and computer efficacy (Likert scale); and − 0.500 between computer efficacy (Likert scale) and computer anxiety (Likert scale). Table 2 (not included in this transcription) shows the means and standard deviations for the dependent variable assessing academic efficacy stated in terms of "items checked," the Likert scale assessing academic efficacy, the Likert scales assessing computer efficacy, and the Likert scale assessing computer anxiety.

In the second study, regression analysis revealed that academic self-efficacy (Likert scale item) accounted for some of the variance in the dependent variable assessing academic efficacy stated in terms of "items checked," $(N = 66, R =. .496, F (1,64) = 20.89, p < .000)$. Computer efficacy (Likert type scale item), $(N = 66, R = .272, F (1, 64) = 5.096, p < .02)$. Computer anxiety (Likert scale item) accounted for some of the variance is computer efficacy (Likert scale item), $(N = 66, R = .500, F (1, 64) = 21.312, p < .000)$.

Study 3 demonstrated the results found during the first study by using one-way ANOVA for those who did not have a computer and by Forms varying in the degrees of human-computer interaction demonstrated significant results, $F (3, 56) = 6.3, p <. .001)$, with academic efficacy (number of items checked) as the dependent variable (Table 3 but not included in the transfer to digital copy).

A Tukey HSD test demonstrated significant results among those who did not have a computer.

The Forms varied in their degree of human-computer interaction, df(56), overall mean = 13.28, p <. . 001, between Form B and Form C, with a mean difference = 5.87, p < .039, between Form C and Form D with a mean difference = - 3.667 (Table 4 but not included in the transfer to digital copy).

Overall, the 2 x 4 (Computer * Form) ANOVA revealed a significant main effect for Form, $F (3,114) = 2.88$, p <. .03), but not for Computer, $F(1,114) = 3.03$, p < .08), or for the interaction Computer * Form, $F (3, 114) = 2.26$, p < .08), with academic efficacy (number of items checked) as the dependent variable. (Table 5 not included in the transfer to digital copy).

Discussion this research demonstrates that the computer is able to influence academic selfefficacy by affecting the number of college academic courses subjects believed they were able to pass. It also demonstrates that among those who do not have a computer, varying the degrees of human-computer interaction can influence academic self-efficacy by affecting the number of college academic courses subjects believed they were able to pass. The first study identified a significant difference in the number of college academic courses subjects believed they were able to pass using a computer and between those who did not have a computer and those who have a computer. The third study identified significant differences in the number of courses subjects believed they were able to pass as a result of varying the degrees of human-computer interaction among those who did not have a computer.

The second study demonstrated that a relationship exists between the number of academic courses subjects believed they could pass using a computer and a belief in their ability to pass, 2) a relationship exists between academic efficacy, computer efficacy, computer anxiety, and 3) computer anxiety plays a role in whether a subject has a computer; and as a result influences computer efficacy.

The second study results demonstrate that: 1) a correlation of. .496 was associated with the initial dependent variable for academic efficacy, "items checked," and the Likert scale item assessing academic efficacy, 2) a negative correlation of -.500 was associated with the Likert scale measure of computer anxiety and the Likert scale assessment of computer efficacy, and 3) a correlations of .272 was associated with the Likert scale measure of computer efficacy and the Likert scale measure of academic efficacy.

These correlations from the second study were significant concerning: 1) the dependent variable "items checked" and the Likert scale of academic efficacy $F(1, 64) = 20.89$, $p <. .000$), 2) the Likert scale assessing computer anxiety and the Likert scale assessing computer efficacy $F(1, 64) = 21.31$, $p < .000$), and 3) the Likert scale assessing computer efficacy and the Likert scale assessing academic efficacy $F(1,64) = 5.096$, $p < .02$).

The results of Study 3, for those who did not have a computer, demonstrated that by varying the degrees of human-computer interaction in academic courses, the number of courses subjects believed they were able to pass varied significantly between Forms B and C, and between Forms C and D. The results of Study 2, assessing information toward explaining the findings of Study 1, suggest that academic efficacy, computer anxiety and computer self-efficacy might be responsible for these differences. It also might be explained by asking a different question: Did a subject: 1) own their computer, and 2) do you have access to a computer, instead of asking "do you have a computer?"

The results of Study 2 demonstrated that the Likert item assessing computer efficacy accounted for 27% of the variance in the Likert scale item assessing academic efficacy. This finding could be the result of the varying degrees of human-computer interaction in different Forms used throughout the overall study, or of having a computer. However, it raises potential questions concerning current academic performance appraisal methods because or implies that subjects may becoming dependent upon their computer skills to supplement their academic ability. If they are depending upon their computer skills to demonstrate their academic ability, are the current academic appraisal methods actually reflecting a student's true level of academic ability?

It is possible that some students might be becoming dependent upon the computer to perform academically, to reach some predetermined level of acceptability? Is it possible, without a computer, or the aid of a computer, that a student may not be able to achieve this predetermined level of acceptability? Is it possible academic human-computer interaction causes a ceiling effect to occur? This, might be a possibility because significant differences between subjects were not found in the dependent variable, number of "items checked," or as a result of varying the degrees of humancomputer interaction throughout the study for those who did have a computer $F(3, 58) = .10$, $p < .05$).

It is beyond the scope of this investigation to answer these questions. Future investigations may choose to ascertain the defining characteristics of academic ability, the potential of a ceiling effect in academic ability when computers are used in the classroom, and the possibility that we are developing a generation that is computer dependent concerning academic ability. Pp 29-37.

This quoted from The Offensiveness of Religion (Brunau, 2019).

Kubler-Ross (1970) identifies five stages the individual experiences in the death of a 'significant other', loved ones, or 'self.' They include: Denial and Isolation, Anger, Bargaining, Depression, and Acceptance. It is not clear the actual time table for these stages, they could most like occur on a sliding scale, moving back and forth, simultaneously or independent of one another. Denial she describes as a barrier that serves to protect the individual(s) after the unexpected and shocking news of a fatal event. This is necessary a function in the human being allowing him to gather himself, with time, to gather other less 'radical' defenses for the psyche. It is usually a temporary defense for the psyche and is soon replaced by a 'partial' acceptance of the events. It is at some point after the individual moves into a process of 'isolationism,' which is characterized by being able to discuss the event with a degree of objectivity, although it is in essence a 'detachment' from the psyche. The death occurred, albeit between a state of reality and fantasy, some degree of acceptance has stepped in. In an effort of being able to cope, the individual has to seemingly separate themselves from the event, separate from the self, separate from the psyche. This is an extremely vulnerable state for any human being. It is a state of confusion, not quite in touch with the self and being removed at the same time, seeking a direction, anything to relieve the confusion.

The second stage she identifies is anger. This stage of anger results from the individual being unable to maintain the state of denial and isolation any longer.

Anger is a difficult stage for the family, friends, and co-workers to cope with. Frequently, this anger is sent out into all directions being cast upon others, the environment, anything in its path without any seeming rationale to or for it. This random executing of the emotion of anger goes outward, those individuals who become inadvertently the target of this misplaced anger in turn respond with their own anger. This back and forth of bouts of anger escalates between those involved in the circumstance and it is often taken personally by mistake. It results in the family, friends, and co-workers using avoidance and shorter periods of interaction with the stricken individual(s), creating an actual state of increased isolation for the person(s) in this state of despair.

The third stage she identifies is bargaining. She explains this is a less known aspect of the process. The individual(s) who were unsuccessful in being able to confront the sadness surrounding death and unsuccessful in their confrontation with anger during the first stage now begin to turn to 'God.' The individual(s) have gone through a process within their mind, toiled with emotions, and figure if, all these other emotions have failed to resolve their grief, it is perhaps time to start making deals with 'God.' If, 'God' seemed to make the decision it was time for the individual(s) to be taken from earth, then if we perform 'good deeds,' the executioner of our 'significant other(s)' will be avenged for us by 'God.' These behaviors are derived from self-imposed feelings of guilt and the individual(s) are in action to reduce this feeling within themselves.

The fourth stage is depression. This is the point when denial has failed, anger and rage no longer suffice, numbness enters and the individual(s) begin to feel they have lost something greater. They might begin to falter on the job, become unable to function, thing start to fall apart. This is a significant turning point for the individual(s). This is a double edged sword for the individual(s). They are encouraged to look ahead, encouraged to look at the good surrounding them, encourage to see the bright side of things, the 'bad guy' has been 'captured and no longer poses a threat. This is when the state of depression is employed to serve as a means of resurrection from the depths of darkness. It is imperative that individual(s) be allowed to express their anger, their hurt, their sorrow, all those emotions that one experiences at the 'bottom of the barrel.' These emotions form the building blocks for a successful emergence into the final stage identified as acceptance.

Acceptance is a stage which is neither identified with the characteristics of anger or depression concerning the 'fate' of individual(s). It is not even possible to make the claim that this is a state of 'happiness.' It is merely a place where 'pain' no longer hurts, there is no 'struggle,' there is perhaps 'nothingness.' There seem to be no emotions having a greater weight to pull the individual(s) in one direction or the other. The individual(s) have exhausted every possible path available to them to resolve their loss, finally they just 'accept' it. It becomes something outside of their own control.

The idea of a significant other has been introduced but has yet to be described. Rosenberg and Turner (1981) suggest significant others are able to affect our self-concept. There are two foundations of interpersonal significance which are related to this affect of self-concept, valuation and credibility. Valuation suggest it is reasonable to expect that the opinions of those people who matter most to us, whose opinions we care about greatly, should have a stronger effect on our self-concept and motivation than the views of whom we are indifferent (i.e., mothers, fathers, siblings, teachers, friends, classmates, chief, priest, pastor, bishop, cardinal, Pope, God). Credibility, another aspect of 'significant other,' suggest the impact of the other's opinion of us also depends on the degree of faith, trust, or confidence that we repose in that person's judgment (i.e., mothers, fathers, siblings, teachers, friends, classmates, chief, priest, pastor, bishop, cardinal, Pope, God). With regard to parents, teachers, and best friends the relationship between the reflected self and the self-concept was stronger if the child had a high faith in the other person's knowledge of the self than if he had low faith. pp. 11

Meeting Elroy and Rosie

Hintze (2016) discusses four types of Artificial Intelligence identified as Reactive Machines, Limited Memory, Theory of Mind, and Self-Awareness. Reactive Machines are the most common Mastery Learning, Behavioral Model, "if-then-else" source code, stimulus-response learning model. It is the most common and described as similar to playing Jeopardy. Limited Memory is a bit more advanced because it can use "time and space" in its model, providing data feeds for self-driving cars. The "Theory of Mind" AI is a psychology term applied to create a machine that can experience feeling, emotion, or create societies (For example, the free game on-line Forge of Empires). Finally, Self-Awareness AI is the attempt by "machines to create machines" that can re-create themselves. There is a philosophical debate and divide whether AI should be creating with the Theory of Mind or Self-Aware abilities. The author (Hintze) was excited to have an acknowledgment regarding the importance of AI in the <u>New White House Report on Artificial Intelligence</u>, attempting to access the link from the on-line article 14 January 2020, the results in Figure 14 and found again at this URL: https://scherlund.blogspot.com/2016/11/understanding-four-types-of-artificial.html .

Regardless, an educational game or any AI is highly dependent on the database as its source to function. Ohrstrom and Hasle (2009) describe in more detail how the database can be one-way tables, two-way tables, or multi-way tables. A one-way table is generally a Relational Database, and a two-way is more often used to identify frequency observations. The data in these tables used to perform statistical analysis, determine frequencies, or indicate a particular domain. It can be visual, like pivot tables or cross tab data evaluation. Bitcoin is nothing more than a distributed linked list database. It is written in the language of C or C++ (Brunau, 2018). Block-chain encryption will enable AI's Theory of Mind or Self-Aware abilities and secure our Personal Data Record (PDR).

Figure 21: The New White House Report on Artificial Intelligence, https://www.whitehouse.gov/sites/default/files/whitehouse_files/microsites/ostp/NSTC/preparing_for_the_future_of_ai.pdf

Relational databases are often MySql, MariaDB, or Oracle named Data Base Management System. They are created by telling a story about Football, Flying a Drone, or a Bike Rental Business. You break the information into parts (Nouns and Verbs). The Nouns in your descriptive paragraph identify the Entity, and the verbs "might have" or "must-have" determine their "relationship cardinality" within the database. Relationship cardinality determines data insertion, updates, or deletion. This relational database development description is quite simplistic as the engine of Artificial Intelligence (AI). Recall the eCHIRPS screenshots?

If you are looking to the future, what kind of things might be possible using technology? This site accessed on 3 June 2020 http://www.nbcnews.com/id/6237364/ns/health-health_care/t/fda-approves-computer-chip-humans#.XsvJ1cBOk2y, the headline exclaims the FDA approved computer chips for humans in 2004. It might be possible to use a 3D printer to create clothing or body parts. Perhaps, the idea of a transitional predictive model for medical health care systems (Howard, 2015). The use of thought to control computer systems and the merging of AI with Humans are on the horizon. Alternatively, the use of computers to control thought? Currently, your identity is a digital score (PDR), according to the Future Today Institute created by Amy Webb and associates.

Webb (2019) indirectly presents a hypothetical case supporting Citizen's United due to its significance in AI. The nine majors in AI create the acronym G-MAFIA (Google, Microsoft, Amazon, Facebook, IBM, and Apple) or BAT (Baidu, Alibaba, and Tencent), where West meets East. The mining algorithms that enable Nation's to defend themselves through data prediction models, provide medical diagnosis and treatment in half the time, or even smart homes increasing leisure time for the family unit. The book seems to suggest the algorithms at work in AI are response based.

For example, a social media post that creates an opposing view amplifies itself and increases the speed of identifying, locating, and posting more articles of similar substance, increasing attention and CPU resources. It is a small snowball rolling down the mountain, getting larger until it creates an avalanche. For example, the conceptual idea of "Track, Identify, Treat," involving the

U0FSUy0yLUNvVg== Virus rose in my consciousness while reading the capabilities of AI. Since AIOOP is describing objects, humans can identify to for ease of programming. Hypothetically, U0FSUy0yLUNvVg== can be a computer virus affecting the medical and health care systems. It would be reasonable for Governments to create an alternative narrative to prevent panic. The HIPPA laws are designed to protect and prevent the lawful release of individual medical records and related information. Remember Stuxnet, in June 2010 with its discovery, a 500-kilobyte computer worm infecting the software of industrial sites in Iran, including a uranium-enrichment plant. The use of AI to manipulate, replicate, and create the virus; and create a vaccine for that virus (Zeldovich, L., 2018) is entirely possible.

Coded internal "bots" continue writing posts to Twitter or Facebook on their own; the AI machine is capable of thought. "Bots" are not necessarily capable of making appropriate judgment calls resulting in saving the crew and passengers aboard Flight 1549. The G-MAFIA or BAT Tribes, predominantly and traditionally male, are a zeitgeist, a by-product of the decades of grooming computer science students in select Colleges and Universities (Webb, 2019). Wu et al. (2017) determined that friends and spouses do have similar characteristics like education, interest, and personality, giving validity to the statement "birds of a feather."

Brunau (2018, 2019, 2020) describes functional projection, the general and specific significant other, and learning theories. Investing or purchasing any cryptocurrency should require reading the corresponding "White Paper." John McAfee of Anti-Virus fame, PowWow developer, Cryptocurrency Entropy Guru, MGTI enterprises, escape from Belize notoriety suggests everyone should read a cryptocurrency's "White Paper." Encryption begins with something like an ASCII, Hex, Binary, Decimal, Base64 converter.

For example, The functional projection process examines the source code, people who create the source code, their bias, their motives, their beliefs, and their values as it correlates with the "White Paper."

Webb (2019) presents Conway's Law suggesting computer systems are the reflection of their creator. AI exists currently without a formal set of ethics, guidelines, or rules to address the "hidden cognitive bias" written in the source code. Code encryption could hypothetically be the chemical interaction enabling personal AI tutors, access Internet of Things (IoT) permission levels, the individual PDR, or securing our private data.

The computer and the use of IoT equipment to perform or complete a task influencing an individual's self-concept is a broad definition of a significant other. Consider years ago, the loss of data or your computer would leave you processing through Kubler-Ross Stages of Death (Brunau, 2020). Recently, research can demonstrate "obedience" in virtual environments and development of trust on-line (Iyer et al. 2020). Slater et al. (2006) re-examined the Milgram Obedience Study. The background, methodology, and conclusion of their study are quoted here:

"Background.

Stanley Milgram's 1960s experimental findings that people would administer apparently lethal electric shocks too stranger at the behest of an authority figure remain critical for understanding obedience. Yet, due to the ethical controversy that his experiments ignited, it is nowadays impossible to carry out direct experimental studies in this area. In the study reported in this paper, we have used a similar paradigm to the one used by Milgram within an immersive virtual environment. Our objective has not been the study of obedience in itself, but of the extent to which participants would respond to such an extreme social situation as if it were real in spite of their knowledge that no real events were taking place.

Methodology.

Following the style of the original experiments, the participants were invited to administer a series of word association memory tests to the (female) virtual human representing the stranger. When she gave an incorrect answer, the participants were instructed to administer an 'electric shock' to her, increasing the voltage each time. She responded with increasing discomfort and protests, eventually demanding termination of the experiment. Of the 34 participants, 23 saw and heard the virtual human, and 11 communicated with her only through a text interface.

Conclusions.

Our results show that in spite of the fact that all participants knew for sure that neither the stranger nor the shocks were real, the participants who saw and heard her tended to respond to the situation at the subjective, behavioral and physiological levels as if it were real. This result reopens the door to direct empirical studies of obedience and related extreme social situations, an area of research that is otherwise not open to experimental study for ethical reasons, through the employment of virtual environments."

Gonzalez-Franco et al. (2018) again replicating Milgram's Studies through virtual reality, examining how participants displayed concern for the learners. Interestingly, they note one of the methods to work around the numerous ethical concerns in replicating the

Milgram studies is to use Actors. Here, quoting the article Abstract from this URL,
https://www.ncbi.nlm.nih.gov/pmc/articles/PMC6312327/pdf/pone.0209704.pdf Accessed 6 June 2020.

> "In Milgram's seminal obedience studies, participants' behavior has traditionally been explained as a demonstration of people's tendency to enter into an 'agentic state' when in the presence of an authority figure: They attend only to the demands of that authority and are insensitive to the plight of their victims. There have been many criticisms of this view, but mostly rely on either indirect or anecdotal evidence. In this study (n = 40) are taken through a virtual reality simulation of the Milgram paradigm. Compared to control participants (n = 20) who are not taken through the simulation, those in the experimental conditions are found to attempt to help the Learners more by putting greater emphasis correct word over the incorrect words. We also manipulate the extent to which participants identify with the science of the study and show that high identifiers both give more help, are less stressed, and are less hesitant to press the shock button that low identifiers. We conclude these findings constitute a refutation of the 'agentic state' approach to obedience. Instead we discuss, implications for the alternative approaches such as engaged follower-ship which suggest that obedience is a function of relative identification with the science and with the victim of the study. Finally, we discuss the value of Virtual Reality as a technique for hard-to-study psychological phenomenon. "

Consider again the capability of AI, "synthetic media, hybrid professors, tweeting, bots on Facebook," and database mining techniques using neural network clustering. This combination suggests further it is possible to create a Virtual Reality authority (a teacher) or the emergence of "engaged follower-ship" (class of students) for a virtual, hybrid Professor William James, MD, Philosopher, and Psychologist. *I wonder if George Abbott and William James knew each other since both were at Harvard?*

Webb (2019) explains Quantum computers have more potential, capability, complexity, and more cost associated with the processor development. There is an increased awareness and desire to create a global coalition that ensures the G-MAFIA and BAT encourage ethical and humane development practices in the domain of AI. Recall, there are a philosophical debate and divide concerning whether AI should be enabled with the Theory of Mind or ability of Self-Awareness. I am not currently aware that Artificial Intelligence Object-Oriented Programming (AIOOP) or Artificial Intelligence Procedural Programming (AIPP) exist at this point in time. *Would AIOOP or AIPP attempt to create, replicate, synthesize or imitate God?*

References

Baker, T., Smith, L., Anissa, N. (2019) <u>Educ-AI-tion Rebooted? Exploring the future of artificial intelligence in schools and colleges</u>. URL: https://media.nesta.org.uk/documents/Future_of_AI_and_education_v5_WEB.pdf Accessed 2 January 2020

Barber, K.R., (2001). <u>Effective Implementation of Integrated Learning Systems.</u> A dissertation submitted to the Division of Diversity Studies and Applied Research, College of Professional Studies, The University of West Florida.

Barron, Kenneth & Hulleman, Chris. (2014). <u>Expectancy-Value-Cost Model of Motivation.</u> 10.1016/B978-0-08-097086-8.26099-6.

Brunau, Erik A. (2018). <u>Bitcoin (BTC): The Art of Artificial Intelligence Warfare</u> Available on Amazon for Kindle

Brunau, Erik A. (2019). <u>The Offensiveness of Religion: Guiding Principles</u> Available on Amazon for Kindle

Brunau, Erik A. (2020). <u>Guns, Games, Education or Legislation: Computer Based Games (CBG), Internet Video Games (IVG), Collaborative Virtual Environments (CVE) and Artificial Intelligence</u> Available on Amazon Kindle

Campbell, Jennifer D.,Trapnell, Paul D.,Heine, Steven J.,Katz, Ilana M.,Lavallee, Loraine F.,Lehman, Darrin R. (1996). <u>Self-concept clarity: Measurement, personality correlates, and cultural boundaries</u>. Journal of Personality and Social Psychology, Vol 70(1), Jan 1996, 141-156

Ferla, J., Valcke, M., and Cai, Y. (2009). <u>Academic self-efficacy and academic self-concept: Reconsidering structural relationships.</u> Learning and Individual Differences, Volume 19, Issue 4, December 2009, Pages 499-505

Gonzalez-Franco, M., Slater, M., Birney, M. E., Swapp, D., Haslam, S. A., & Reicher, S. D. (2018). <u>Participant concerns for the Learner in a Virtual Reality replication of the Milgram obedience study.</u> *PloS one, 13*(12), e0209704. https://doi.org/10.1371/journal.pone.0209704

Granic, I., Lobel, A., Engels, R. (2014). <u>The Benefits of Playing Video Games</u>, American Psychologist, January, Vol 69, No.1, 66-78

Hintze, Arend (2016). <u>Understanding the Four Types of Artificial Intelligence,</u> Government Technology, Cloud & Computing, https://www.govtech.com/computing/Understanding-the-Four-Types-of-Artificial-Intelligence.html Accessed 14 January 2020

Howard, Jacqueline (2015). <u>7 Top Futurists Make Some Pretty Surprising Predictions About What The Next Decade Will Bring</u>, https://www.huffpost.com/entry/futurists-next-10-years_n_7241210, Accessed 23 May 2020

Iyer, S., Cheng, J., Brown, N., Wang, X. (2020). When Does Trust in Online Social Groups Grow? https://research.fb.com/wp-content/uploads/2020/05/When-Does-Trust-in-Online-Social-Groups-Grow.pdf Accessed 28 June 2020

Khenissi, M.A., Essalmi, F., Jemni, M., Kinshuk, S.B., Chen, N. (2016). <u>Relationship Between Learning Styles and Genres of Games, Computers & Education 101</u>, pp 1-14, https://www.journals.elsevier.com/computers-and-education, available online 19 May 2016

Kosinski, Michal, Stillwell, David, and Graepel, Thore (2013). Private traits and attributes are predictable from digital records of human behavior URL: https://www.pnas.org/content/110/15/5802.full Accessed 3 June 2020

Lee, Chiawen; Aiken, Kirk Damon; Hung, Huang Chia (2012). Effects of College Students' Video Gaming Behavior on Self-Concept Clarity and Flow, Social Behavior and Personality: an international journal, Volume 40, Number 4, 2012, pp. 673-679(7) URL: https://www.ingentaconnect.com/

Luckin, Rose; Holmes, Wayne; Griffiths, Mark and Forcier, Laurie B. (2016).Intelligence Unleashed: An Argument for AI in Education. Pearson Education, London.

Matz, S.C., Kosinski, M., Nave, G., and Stillwell, D.J. (2017). Psychological targeting as an effective approach to digital mass persuasion. URL: https://www.pnas.org/content/114/48/12714 Accessed 3 June 2020

McLeod, S. A. (2018, Aug 05). *Lev Vygotsky*. Simply Psychology. https://www.simplypsychology.org/vygotsky.html

Accessed 18 December 2019.

Millman, R. (2018). Scientists develop A.I. to predict why children do badly at school. Internet of Business, URL: https://internetofbusiness.com/scientists-develop-ai-to-predict-why-children-do-badly-at-school/ Accessed 1 January 2020

National Center for Education Statistics (2018). The Condition of Education Assessments. Last updated May 2019. URL: https://nces.ed.gov/programs/coe/indicator_snd.asp Accessed 22 December 2019

Ohrstrom, P. & Hasle, P. (2009). <u>Time in Philosophical Logic.</u> URL: https://www.academia.edu/11847300/, Accessed 15 January 2020

Plass, J.L., Homer, B.D., and Kinzer, C.K., (2015). <u>Foundations of Game-Based Learning.</u> Educational Psychologist, 50(4), 258-283

Pleasant, R., Ritzhaupt, A.D., (2013) .<u>Video Games and Learning: Teaching and Participatory Culture in a Digital Age,</u> International Journal of Gaming and Computer-Mediated Simulations, 5(4), 100-102, October-December

Rogers, C. (1959). <u>A theory of therapy, personality and interpersonal relationships as developed in the client-centered framework.</u> In (ed.) S. Koch,*Psychology: A study of a science. Vol. 3: Formulations of the person and the social context.* New York: McGraw Hill.

Rogers, C.R., Lyon Jr., H.C., -4Tausch, R. (2014). <u>On Becoming an Effective Teacher: Person-centered Teaching, Psychology, Philosophy and Dialogues with Carl R. Rogers and Harold Lyon.</u> ISBN: 978-0-415-81698

Slater, M., Antley, A., Davison, A., Swapp, D., Guger, C., Barker, C., Pistrang, N., & Sanchez-Vives, M. V. (2006). <u>A virtual reprise of the Stanley Milgram obedience experiments</u>. *PloS one, 1*(1), e39. https://doi.org/10.1371/journal.pone.0000039

Segalin, C., Celli, F., Polonio, L., Kosinski, M., Stillwell, D., Sebe, N., … Lepri, B. (2017). <u>What your Facebook profile picture reveals about your personality</u>. *Proceedings of the 2017 ACM on Multimedia Conference.*

Stankov, L., Lee, J., Luo, W., Hogan, D. J. (2012). <u>Confidence: A better predictor of academic achievement than self-efficacy, self-concept and anxiety?</u> Learning and Individual Differences Volume 22, Issue 6, December 2012, Pages 747-758 . URL: https://www.sciencedirect.com Accessed 27 December 2019

University at Buffalo (2019). Center for Educational Innovation (CEI). URL: http://www.buffalo.edu/ubcei/learning/studen-motivation/motivation-theories.html Accessed: 30 December 2019

Wang, A.I., Ofsdahl, T., Morch-Sorstein, O.K. (2009). <u>Collaborative Learning Through Games-Characteristics, Models and Taxonomy</u>. Google Scholar, URL: http://citeseerx.ist.psu.edu/viewdoc/download?doi=10.1.1.159.4657&rep=rep1&type=pdf Site Accessed 29 December 2019

Webb, Amy (2016). <u>The Signals are Talking Why Today's Fringe is Tomorrow's Mainstream</u>. Public Affairs Press, ISBN-13: 978-1-5417-8823-7

Webb, Amy (2019). <u>The Big Nine: How Tech Titans and Their Thinking Machines Could Warp Humanity.</u> Public Affairs Press, ISBN:-13:978-1-5417-7373-8

Weiner, B. (2019). Attribution Theory (B.Weiner).

URL: https://www.instructionaldesign.org/theories/attribution-theory/ Accessed 26 December 2019

Weiner, B. (1985). <u>An attributional theory of achievement motivation and emotion</u>, Psychological Review, 92, 548-573.

Wigfield, A., Eccles, J.S. (2000). <u>Expectancy–Value Theory of Achievement Motivation</u>. Contemporary Educational Psychology, 25, 68-81, available online at http://www.idealibrary.com, Accessed 1 January 2020

Wu Youyou, David Stillwell, H. Andrew Schwartz, and Michal Kosinski (2017). <u>Birds of a feather do flock together: Behavior-based personality-assessment method reveals personality similarity among couples and friends</u>. Psychological Science. Psychological Science, 28, 276–284. doi:10.1177/0956797616678187

Yusuf, M.O., & Afolabi, A. (2010). <u>Effects of Computer Assisted Instruction (CAI) on Secondary School Students' Performance in Biology</u>. Available on line accessed 17 December 2019
URL: https://www.semanticscholar.org/paper/Effects-of-Computer-Assisted-Instruction-(CAI)-On-Yusuf-Afolabi/

Zeldovich, Lina (2018). <u>A Virologist's Revolutionary Team Approach to Vaccine Development</u>, Stony Brook University Magazine, 03, Winter, URL: https://www.stonybrook.edu/magazine/2018-winter/a-virologists-revolutionary-team-approach-to-vaccine-development Accessed 5 June 2020

www.ingramcontent.com/pod-product-compliance
Lightning Source LLC
Chambersburg PA
CBHW070758250726
48662CB00004B/1873